W9-BZP-258

3 3277 00208 4650

ADVICE TO
A PLAYER

tectum

porticus

mimorum
ædes

orchestra

sedilia

ingressus

proscænium

plænities fiue arena.

Ex obseruationibus Londinensibus
Johannis de witt

The Swan theater, sketched by
Jan de Witt in 1596

ADVICE TO A PLAYER

A Collection of Monologues from
Shakespeare with Explanatory Notes

by

Donald MacKechnie

Foreword by Joan Plowright

Limelight Editions
New York

Camas Public Library

First Limelight Edition March 2002

Copyright © 2002 by Donald MacKechnie

All rights reserved including the right of reproduction in whole
or in part in any form.
Published by Proscenium Publishers
Inc., 118 East 30th Street, New York, NY 10016.

Manufactured in the United States of America

Library of Congress Cataloging-in-Publication Data

Shakespeare, William, 1564-1616.
Advice to a player : a collection of monologues from
Shakespeare with explanatory notes / Donald Mackechnie ;
foreword by Joan Plowright.— 1st Limelight ed.
p. cm.
ISBN 0-87910-962-9
1. Shakespeare, William, 1564-1616—Quotations.
2. Monologues. 3. Acting. I.
Mackechnie, Donald. II. Title.

PR2768 .M33 2001
822.3'3 — DC21
2001050516

This book is dedicated to
Jose de Jesus Barrera Lara

I WOULD LIKE TO ACKNOWLEDGE BOTH
JON ERIC LEHMAN AND DALE WAYNE SANDLIN
FOR THEIR HELP IN GETTING THIS BOOK TO THE PUBLIC.

Contents

CONTENTS

"A Passion to Tatters"

"Let Discretion Be Your Tutor"

CONTENTS

"Let Those That Play Your Clowns"

Foreword

I have known Donald MacKechnie for many years, ever since we worked together at The National Theatre of Great Britain in the 1960's where he was Staff Producer to my late husband, Laurence Olivier. He has an almost encyclopaedic knowledge of theatre and acting styles, and as a director always enjoyed a tremendous rapport with his actors.

I think he's done an excellent job of de-mystifying Shakespeare in his book. Though he abjures an over-reverential approach to performing Shakespeare, he points out that "Bill" (as he calls him) knew exactly what he was doing as regards the punctuation of texts. MacKechnie explains the rich potential of each of the chosen speeches; gives the background knowledge so that they are anchored in reality and not floating about in a vacuum; and offers expert advice on how to avoid the pitfalls.

"O for a Muse of Fire" (page 11) was the speech I chose when auditioning for the Old Vic years ago. I fell into all the traps we are warned about, and I wish *Advice to a Player* had been around then for me to "read, mark, learn and inwardly digest."

His humorous approach makes the book fun to read, but does not disguise his passionate commitment to helping actors overcome the hurdles, and to spread their wings and fly. No actor attempting his first Shakespearean role (or even his second) should be without it.

Joan Plowright Olivier

A Word or Two Beforehand

Hello!

I have attempted in the following pages to illuminate a number of speeches from the works attributed to William Shakespeare. I hope the suggestions enclosed may help an actor to establish a few base camps from which to scale the various mountains contained in the remainder of the work of this master playwright.

I would like readers to understand that, although I will often refer to William Shakespeare as "Bill," it is not done in any sense of either economy or disrespect. I just happen to believe that, over the years, many of us have allowed this author to become too distant a figure. We have forgotten that Bill, whoever he was, was a mere mortal.

On that last point it is immaterial to me whether the Earl of Oxford, or Lord Stanley, or John Dover Wilson in another life, or Jonson, or Marlowe, or anyone else for that matter, even Queen Elizabeth, wrote these plays. I place myself in the good company, I understand, of Mark Twain, inasmuch as I think the plays were "definitely written by William Shakespeare, or someone calling himself William Shakespeare." All that really matters is that the plays were written, and we must thank the gods, preferably on at least a daily basis, that the writing still has such firm currency today. I will only affirm that it has helped me immeasurably over the years to refer to the writer of Shakespeare's plays as Bill. The use of an abbreviated name has enabled me, sometimes in the dead of night, to "telephone" Bill and to obtain, usually, an immediate response.

Apart from my fantastical telephone communication, there is no doubt in my mind that this author has made himself amazingly available to us all. No secret intention is kept from the actor; everything is clearly laid out, and yet no too-rigid discipline constricts the actor's potential for interpretation. The playwright constantly tells us what he is about; what he wants to happen; how he suggests that it might happen; what has been the effect of the happening. All that is required, I think, is that in order to make the most of the opportunities provided in the text, the actor, contemplating the work, should understand a few simple ground rules.

PUNCTUATION: I hope when I finally meet Bill that he will confirm his intention that his actors breathe on the sentence, not necessarily on the line but at a period, exclamation mark, or question mark. Breaking this rule, occasionally, as all good rules must be broken, for a semicolon, maybe.

Do not underestimate the writer's knowledge of singing and his knowledge of what a well conditioned actor may accomplish on a given breath. It surely seems that he knew about breathing and that the punctuation behind the breathing invariably carries great strength and forward momentum. This is not to say that an actor may speak the text too operatically. Be mindful. The great English actor Sir Donald Wolfit once challenged the distinguished Australian ballet dancer Sir Robert Helpmann when the latter announced that he was going to perform a ballet of *Hamlet.* "You are going to dance Hamlet, Bobby?" "Why not," said Sir Robert. "After all, Donald, you've been singing the role for years." Probably an apocryphal story. but one in which there is a true lesson. There is little worse in theatre than to hear a company pedantically "singing" their way through one of Bill's plays.

ARCHITECTURE: The writer clearly wrote for a specific spatial formula; a specific design of theatre. The open stage, or thrust, was his regular sounding board. We need to understand a little about Elizabethan theatre architecture and to think occasionally about it. Even if the production design at hand bears no resemblance to the shape that was initially used for the play, many puzzles are solved through understanding and appreciating the original space. Those long exits and entrances are easier to handle if we acknowledge that an actor working for Bill was often likely to be seen by some part of the house long before he was actually "in" the scene. The fact that the audience was wrapped around a thrust stage, scattered across some grand palace chamber, or crowded into an inn courtyard forced the actor into a certain naturalism; the proscenium arch, if you are not careful, will do quite the opposite, forcing everything through the fourth wall, through which too much may then appear forced. (See the sketch at the beginning of this book and much will be explained.)

AUDIENCES: Bill seemed to know his audience particularly well. He wrote, and sometimes overwrote, for the various intelligence levels represented by theatregoers of his day with often a triple layering of reason through the plays. There is usually a superior intellectual thrust to appease those educated gentry who found themselves in the closest proximity to the actors, or who were actually sitting on the stage itself upon occasion, or even in some rare cases, depicted in the plot.

The middle ground often argued in the plays was beamed out to the merchants, soldiers, and various other middle classes customarily seated in the main body of the kirk.

Then there is the not to be underestimated, raucous, vulgar side which was usually voiced to keep at arms length the nut-cracking groundlings, who stood, or wandered around in the pit before the stage. (Cinema audiences today have their popcorn; it seems Elizabethan theatre audiences had a predilection for hazel nuts. One trembles to think of the noise that even a few groundlings could make with the cracking of the tasty morsels during a performance. Probably kept the acting company on their toes.)

WHAT ACTORS WAS BILL WRITING FOR: Anyone who knows me will confirm that I am not a male chauvinist, but it has to be acknowledged that this author wrote exclusively for an all male company of players.

Don't panic!

I am not advocating, in any sense, the perpetual continuance of such a style of playing. The gods, to say nothing of several treasured lady friends who happen to be rather brilliant actresses, forbid. I only mention the fact at all because I believe any lady will be more successful in the role of Cleopatra, or Lady Macbeth, Lady Anne, or Rosalind, to name but four, if she acknowledges the circumstances of the writer's times and acts accordingly. I happen to think it can do an actress playing Lady Macbeth, for example, no harm to rehearse for a week or two as a young man. I had some success once with this play, actually deploying a very talented twelve-year-old male named Russel Dixon (now an extremely talented professional actor) in the role of Lady Macbeth in rehearsal. Had I been able at the time to find a similarly talented adolescent young man to play Lady MacDuff, I would have put them both into performance, but I could not and did not. However, the experiment in rehearsal helped the production enormously and not least in the subsequent and quite remarkable portrayal of Lady Macbeth, played by Patricia Doyle, which, I dare to say it, was the best Lady Macbeth I have ever seen. Thank you, Patricia!

Just before you embark on what I hope will be a useful and exciting adventure, I should say that I have used the late John Dover Wilson's Cambridge University Press edition of the plays and that the same editor has edited most of the plays in the Arden editions, should you wish to refer to his specific footnote or glossary. Dover Wilson's style was to use an accented "è" for what he felt should be a positively stressed "ed" ending. I have followed him in this thought.

Be aware: a well punctuated text is most useful. A poorly punctuated text may be misleading and present the actor with many unnecessary problems.

Apropos the actors for whom these plays were originally written, it seems quite likely that most actors were given only their part or their "side;" the one with which they were directly involved, and not, as is now customary, the entire play. Somewhat like working for the illustrious film director Woody Allen, who I understand works in a similar manner.

Despite understanding the early style of rehearsing the plays with "sides" only, no actor or actress should be persuaded that it is a good idea not to read the entire play. There is now no shortage of paper and ink, as there was in Elizabethan England; nor will you find yourself, customarily, acting under the tutelage of Mr Allen, though opportunity would be a fine thing since the man is pushing genius. If you are fortunate enough to find yourself engaged by the eminent New York film director, you must most certainly do as he requests, but if you are engaged in a theatrical representation of any play it behooves you to read the whole script; you will perform much more effectively in your class, your audition, or your theatre production.

I have followed each selected speech with some comments, and then with notes headed WHY, WHERE, WHO, and OTHER. The notes are intended to explain something of why the speech is in the play; where the speech takes place; who the listeners might be; and some other notes which might be relevant. You will doubtless have ideas of your own; I merely hope to start you thinking.

The speeches discussed are fairly equally divided between the sexes, but of course, the ladies reading these pages should consider such speeches as Jaques' "Seven Ages of Man," the Chorus of *Henry V*, the Prologue for *Romeo and Juliet*, and in fact any speech which they feel might serve them well in an audition environment.

As I have already pointed out, the women's roles Portia,

Lady Anne, Lady Macbeth et al were written for male actors in the first instance, so the gentlemen may also take their pick.

Margaret, from *Henry VI, Part 3*, might be a place to start.

Remember, Bill Shakespeare, generally speaking, keeps things very simple. If you follow his leads and guidelines; listen to the clues he drops; investigate the play, and do the right detective work, I am sure you will heighten your enjoyment of the pieces.

Onward!

"SPEAK THE SPEECH"

I see those in this first section as more or less declamatory "speeches." They are not interpretive monologues, rather they are outgoing, advisory, informative, or expositional speeches.
You will see what I mean, I hope.

HAMLET

HAMLET Act 3, Scene 2.
The hall of the castle.
Enter Hamlet and three of the Players

Hamlet: Speak the speech I pray you as I pronounced it to you, trippingly on the tongue, but if you mouth it as many of your players do, I had as lief the town-crier spoke my lines. Nor do not saw the air too much with your hand thus, but use all gently, for in the very torrent, tempest, and as I may say whirlwind of your passion, you must acquire and beget a temperance that may give it smoothness. O, it offends me to the soul, to hear a robustious periwig-pated fellow tear a passion to tatters, to very rags, to split the ears of the groundlings, who for the most part are capable of nothing but inexplicable dumb-shows and noise: I would have such a fellow whipped for o'erdoing Termagant, it out-herods Herod, pray you avoid it.

3

(1 PLAYER: I warrant your honor.)

Hamlet: Be not too tame neither, but let your own discretion be your tutor, suit the action to the word, the word to the action, with this special observance, that you o'erstep not the modesty of nature: for anything so o'erdone is from the purpose of playing, whose end both at the first, and now, was and is, to hold as 'twere the mirror up to nature, to show virtue her own feature, scorn her own image, and the very age and body of the time his form and pressure... Now this overdone, or come tardy off, though it make the unskillful laugh, cannot but make the judicious grieve, the censure of the which one must in your allowance o'erweigh a whole theatre of others. O there be players that I have seen play - and heard others praise, and that highly - not to speak it profanely, that neither having th'accent of Christians, nor the gait of Christian, pagan, nor man, have so strutted and bellowed, that I have thought some of nature's journeymen had made men, and not made them well, they imitated humanity so abominably.

(1 PLAYER: I hope we have reformed that indifferently with us, sir.)

Hamlet: (O reform it altogether,) and let those that play your clowns speak no more than is set down for them, for there be of them that will themselves laugh, to set on some quantity of barren spectators to laugh too, though in the meantime some necessary question of the play be then to be considered. That's villainous, and shows a most pitiful ambition in the fool that uses it... Go make you ready.

NB. (Delete bracketed lines for audition)

This sequence from Hamlet talking with the Players who have newly arrived in Elsinore depicts not only a Prince of Denmark but, more important for our purposes, an established man of the theatre and moreover a man who knows good acting. If the job had been invented then, which it most definitely was not, Hamlet might have made a good theatre director. Here he is quietly giving the cast a pep talk, or as is sometimes said, Hamlet is giving his "Advice to the Players."

All of Hamlet's notes in this speech, if properly adhered to, will create a most complete actor. It is appropriate that it is the first piece I suggest to you as I hold it to embrace every acting note anyone could require for a full career in the professional theatre. The general advice on acting given within this speech may, obviously, be applied to every monologue in this book. I think if an actor is comfortable with "The Advice," and can go on to demonstrate its message, the resulting work can only be very good.

A few thoughts about studying the delivery of this text.

Think about "trippingly," about "mouthing," and think about "town criers," with their boring repetition of "Oh, yes! Oh, yes! Twelve o'clock and all's well!" and the like.

Think about the tendency to let your hands work overtime. Watch the economy of the great Burton, Gielgud, Hayes, Hepburn, Pacino, Plowright, Redgrave (Michael), Smith (Maggie).

Think about tempering your passion. You cannot take an audience with you if your anger, or any other emotion, descends, or for that matter, ascends, to incoherence.

Particularly if you are reading this in a school, college, university, or within striking distance of Equity Waiver

Theatre in Los Angeles, think about playing to the lowest common denominator, and then decide against doing so.

BIG NOTE. "Let your own discretion be your tutor." You are acting the play, or, in this instance, performing the audition. Do seek advice from others around you, but do not allow yourself to be "directed" into an attitude of playing with which you are not comfortable. When you can, avoid being "directed" at all costs. "Directing" in the theatre is a frighteningly modern invention, and something which I think almost solely benefits "Directors." I write as one who has directed more than two hundred professional productions in various theatres around the world and, like Noel Coward, all I ask is that you "be careful." In fact, possibly the only mistake in the illustrious career of the great actor William Charles Macready was to give the English–speaking theatre the idea that an "El Supremo" was at all necessary. Even then (in the mid-Nineteenth Century) they were only Producers. Since the early twentieth century we have allowed ourselves to accept Directors (it is usually they who insist on the capital "D"). Far too often, in theatre, directors run amok; keep in mind that the theatre did quite well without directors for a few thousand years.

Be aware of "the modesty of nature." Simplicity is everything.

Really think about "the judicious grieve," that one imaginary person an actor may always place in the audience and for whom he may perform the play. Hang onto that. The lesson is primary to all good acting. This "judicious" person does not need to exist in reality. There is nothing "real" about good theatre. There is only dramatic reality and dramatic reality is usually light years removed from reality. In the twilight world of theatrical reality, you may, as a respectable actor, be allowed to fantasize the perfect foil for your playing on any particular evening. Tomorrow, or at the next audition, it may be that you will use some other image.

Finally, do think about Bill's brilliant advice on the art of comedy: the cautionary words about ad-libbing: The thought that too much laughter is not always a good thing, even for comedy, and it is never good if the laughter distracts from the audience's understanding of the play.

It was once my privilege to work with the great French actor and director Jacques Charon,

I once sat with him in the stalls as he watched a run-through of a farce he had directed for the company a few years previously. At the end of the third act he said "It is very, very good, but there are now too many laughs in the first act." M.Charon was, of course, quite right: there were "necessary questions of the play," at that time (in Act 1) "to be considered."

What else?

Only to say that the whole scene has an inner buoyancy and sense of enjoyment for me, keyed off that first line and the use of the words "trippingly on the tongue." If you decide to play around with the idea of one breath for a sentence you will, even if you have the lungs of Placido Domingo, be forced, in this speech, into a certain rapidity and lightness of touch.

You will, as Hamlet, be talking in a kindly, discreet, and humorous manner to your cast, which is precisely what a good director should do, particularly prior to a first performance.

WHY: Hamlet is being a kind host and greeting a touring company, who have unexpectedly arrived at Elsinore. Clearly it is a happenstance that the actors have arrived at this moment and brought a breath of life to a castle in mourning. Though it is not referred to in this passage, the young prince sees a way of attacking the king, his uncle, through the device of inserting some pertinent material into a play soon to be performed by the newly arrived group of players. It suits Hamlet's purposes here to be intelligent with the cast and to make sure that they carry off the play well, and more to the point, his insertion of "some dozen or sixteen lines or so." "The plays the thing" wherein Hamlet hopes to "catch the conscience of the king." Hamlet is convinced that his uncle, now King Claudius, is a usurper and a murderer, guilty not only of regicide, but also of fratricide.

Hamlet seems to care passionately about good theatre. He seems to enjoy himself here very much indeed and his notes and ideas are so flawless that we might well think that the Prince of Denmark has clearly missed his vocation in not putting them more quickly into practice. As he demonstrates repeatedly throughout the play, Hamlet knows what he is talking about and is clearly a fine actor.

WHERE: A room in the castle at Elsinore? In the reality for which the play was written, it might be a somewhat cold and dark room. Probably a Great Hall, into which a platform, or a "scaffold," might be introduced for the players. Time of day is not specific. The players could arrive in the late forenoon, or the afternoon, to make ready for the evening.

WHO: Hamlet is talking to an audience of itinerant actors, but the actor playing Hamlet originally (we think Richard Burbage) would have to be aware that he was also talking to an audience of theatregoers who might well be very familiar with his subject matter. Such might not be the case today. The actor playing Hamlet in the twenty-first century may not, regrettably, expect his audience to be so well versed in matters of theatre.

OTHER: What does Hamlet hope to achieve? A good play well delivered, in which his barbed insertion is deftly hidden. What does the actor playing Hamlet hope to achieve? A good play well delivered, in which his performance is deftly accomplished. It is a charismatic scene really, which will, if properly played, endear the character and the actor to their respective audiences, or the auditionee to the casting director or producer.

Glossary

LIEF willingly.

TOWN CRIER minor local government official who walks the streets declaring the time of day or night, and announcing any news that might affect the general populace.

PERIWIG a form of wig.

PATE(D) head.

GROUNDLINGS audience members who, in Elizabethan theatres, usually stood (on the ground) for the duration of the play.

DUMB SHOWS a pantomime, or "dumb show," out-
lining the plot, which often preceded a performance.

TERMAGANT angry Muslim deity, featured in some
medieval morality plays.

HEROD Yes, that Herod, who attempted to kill all
the firstborn male children.

GAIT stride or pattern of walking.

CHORUS

HENRY V Act 1, Scene 1.

Prologue: Enter Chorus

Chorus: O for a muse of fire, that would ascend
The brightest heaven of invention:
A kingdom for a stage, princes to act,
And monarchs to behold the swelling scene.
Then should the warlike Harry, like himself,
Assume the port of Mars, and at his heels,
Leashed in like hounds, should Famine, Sword,
    and Fire
Crouch for employment. But pardon, gentles all,
The flat unraisèd spirits that hath dared
On this unworthy scaffold to bring forth
So great an object. Can this cockpit hold
The vasty fields of France? or may we cram
Within this wooden O the very casques

That did affright the air at Agincourt?
O, pardon! Since a crooked figure may
Attest in little place a million;
And let us, ciphers to this great accompt,
On your imaginary forces work....
Suppose within the girdles of these walls
Are now confined two mighty monarchies,
Whose high upreared and abutting fronts
The perilous narrow ocean parts asunder.
Piece out our imperfections with your thoughts:
Into a thousand parts divide one man,
And make imaginary puissance.
Think, when we talk of horses, that you see them
Printing their proud hoofs i'th' receiving earth:
For 'tis your thoughts that now must deck our
    kings,
Carry them here and there: jumping o'er times;
Turning th'accomplishment of many years
Into an hour-glass: for the which supply,
Admit me Chorus to this history;
Who prologue-like your humble patience pray,
Gently to hear, kindly to judge, our play.

Well, what about that?

This, the opening speech of *Henry V*, spoken by the Chorus, is of course a famous yardstick, but for an audition piece it is loaded with display potential. The ability to charm is here; the earnest apologies of the Chorus on behalf of his theatre company require an expert touch; the necessity to paint a picture, to rouse and then to settle an audience in almost the same breath. The actor or actress using the Chorus for an audition should be capable of exercising the fullest control. This speech is not merely technically involved; the actor may be emotionally involved to a degree and involve, on an emotional level, those before whom he or she plays the speech. In a performance, of course, the chorus will set the tone for the entire production.

I believe that the primary responsibility of a good actor is to be of good service to the other actors. We are each here to serve our colleagues, and nowhere is this ability to serve better expressed than in this prologue. To step out here and herald the following history, the actor playing this chorus must love his colleagues. The Chorus has a huge duty to the production and an obligation to the remainder of the cast, particularly when one acknowledges that Henry V is not one of Bill's better efforts. (Even in his time the play must have come off as a little too jingoistic and the subject of *Henry V* had, even then, been done to death.)

The excitement the actor portrays for the play ahead should be highly charged, reminiscent perhaps of the pulsating energy that erupts from the orchestra pit during the overture of a Broadway musical. Tempering the charge, however, is the necessity to keep the speech open, and moving forward; to begin with the roundest of vowels and continue in an almost operatic manner. Be careful!

This opening speech by the Chorus is also a great tool for learning, in that it embraces many images of true theatre, which seem too often to be denied. I mean that it asks from the audience a great deal. This Chorus knows and admits that he does not have the production values of Aaron Spelling behind him, and that the play may be enjoyed only through the congregation lending itself fully to the work of the actors.

If you haven't already done so, or even if you have, do

read Hamlet's advice to the players (see page 2) in relation to this speech. (I'll stop saying that soon, but not yet.)

WHY: It is imperative for the audience in the theatre to be presented with a lens through which they may view this play. This prologue is at once an apology for the sparseness of theatre and a celebration of how good theatre may be well accomplished with the aid of the audience. The tone of the evening will be set with the speaking of this one speech. If the speech is well played, we will know for the rest of the evening where to look for the play and how to listen for the play. This is the tour guide introducing us to the evening. This is the Chorus appealing to the child within us all, the child who used to be able to enjoy a game of let's pretend.

WHERE: It is self-explanatory, isn't it? See the rendering of the Rose Theatre at the beginning of this book. The wooden O, the scaffold, and so on. Peter Brook writes that a theatre is "an empty space through which someone walks whilst someone else is watching." That is really precisely what the Chorus is saying here.

WHO: It can be difficult for modern actors, as we are not so used to addressing the audience directly. Here the Chorus lives or dies by the contact he may establish at the outset. It really is Leno and Letterman doing their bit of stand-up at the beginning of those late-night shows. Leno is quite a good role model in, some ways, for the attitude of the Chorus. I suspect Mr. Leno is not a great verse speaker, but he knows this area of expertise: How goes the monologue, so goes the show.

OTHER: What is to be accomplished is an understanding on the part of the audience that they are an integral and participatory part of the playing of the play. In relation to an audition, you have ample opportunity to display your wares and to encourage those who are before you to think.

Glossary

HARRY a derivative of Henry.

PORT OF MARS image of the god of war.

LEASHED IN as hunting dogs, often held to the last moment before being released.

SCAFFOLD wooden structure/ stage.

CASQUE(S) headdress of armor.

AGINCOURT castle in France, after which the Battle of Agincourt was named. Grossly outnumbered, Henry V won the day with far superior strategy and through the brilliant deployment and use of his yeomen and their lethal longbows. October 25, 1415.

CROOKED FIGURE symbol for one million.

ACCOMPT account.

NARROW OCEAN English Channel.

PUISSANCE power.

LADY MACBETH

MACBETH Act 1, Scene 5.
Inverness. Macbeth's castle.
Enter Macbeth's wife alone, with a letter

Lady Macbeth (*reads*): "They met me in the day of success; and I have learned by the perfect'st report, they have more in them than mortal knowledge. When I burned in desire to question them further, they made themselves air, into which they vanished.

"Whiles I stood rapt in the wonder of it, came missives from the king, who all-hailed me, 'Thane of Cawdor,' by which title, before, these Weird Sisters saluted me, and referred me to the coming on of time, with 'Hail, king that shalt be!'

"This have I thought good to deliver thee (my dearest partner in greatness) that thou mightst not lose the dues of rejoicing, by being ignorant of what greatness is promised thee.

"Lay it to thy heart, and farewell."
Glamis thou art, and Cawdor, and shalt be
What thou art promised: yet do I fear thy nature,
It is too full o'th' milk of human kindness
To catch the nearest way: thou wouldst be great,
Art not without ambition, but without
The illness should attend it: what thou wouldst
    highly,
That wouldst thou holily; wouldst not play false,
And yet wouldst wrongly win: thou'ldst have, great
    Glamis,
That which cries 'Thus thou must do', if thou have it,
And that which rather thou dost fear to do
Than wishest should be undone. Hie thee hither,
That I may pour my spirits in thine ear,
And chastise thee with the valour of my tongue
All that impedes thee from the golden round,
Which fate and metaphysical aid doth seem
To have thee crowned withal.

Here, with Lady Macbeth reading the letter from her
long absent husband, is an opportunity to demonstrate
grace, agility, youth, seductiveness, intelligence, ambition,
wifely devotion, zest for life, and that is just in reaction to
the letter itself.

Breaking into "Glamis thou art," an actor is able to release the introduction to the darker side of Lady Macbeth,
but even in the exhibitory nature of an audition piece, and
certainly in the playing of the play, one should be careful
not to go too far too soon. Unquestionably, Lady Macbeth
is raising the image of her absent husband in this response
to the letter.

For what it is worth, to the best of our knowledge, the actual Lady Macbeth was, although previously married, a young teenager at the time of her marriage to the Thane of Glamis. Think of yourself as an adolescent girl in this, perhaps, awe-inspiring position.

Speaking of Lady Macbeth's age prompts me to say that in my opinion the time frame of this play is not much short of chronic, so much appears hurried. The murder of Duncan seems to follow on the heels of the first battle; Macbeth is crowned; Banquo killed; Malcolm arrives; the whole process seems only a matter of weeks, and not the years it was. As a consequence, it doesn't come easily to age these two bizarrely written images of Scottish nobility, the Thane of Cawdor and his wife. Again as a matter of fact, they were married for some considerable time. Indeed, Macbeth reigned for about seventeen years. In theory that indicates to me that the younger you can get the role of Lady Macbeth at the start, the better will be the journey you are able to make in the character; the more understandable will be her drive for position and power, and her fall from both.

Lady Macbeth is reasoning very well here at the outset, if a little too enthusiastically.

The author is setting her up for a great demise, however, through which she will finally descend to insanity and over the battlements to her death.

WHY: We have seen so far in the play only the war-torn side of Scotland, and, as it happens, even including the witches, the more masculine side. Here is the so-called weaker sex, flashing onto the stage with letter in hand and in a state of high expectation and some anxiety. We should see that there is enormous potential in this young woman who has a good brain and who is highly motivated sexually.

WHERE: Not specific in the text, and it must be at the discretion of the actor. The scene could be set outside in the grounds of Glamis Castle, or in a state room or other chamber of some kind. Perhaps Lady Macbeth is ripping a fax from the machine in the estate office.

WHO: Unlike the Chorus in *Henry V*, this lady is alone. Lady Macbeth is not actually addressing the audience in the way that the *Henry V* Chorus must. It might be a choice of the actor's to include the audience in some way, of course, but in fact, Lady M. has some of her most private moments here, in the receipt of this, to her, amazing letter.

OTHER: What does the character establish? Initially there is some bond of understanding made with the voyeuristic audience watching her. It is possible, with the playing of the letter, to show the audience the bright young wife who has been absent from her husband for too long. Another thought, though it is not necessarily relevant to this scene. It is most likely that this very young woman, already twice married, did give birth in her first marriage. Lady Macbeth's later line "I have given suck," leads some people to imagine that she must be an older woman, but one has only to look at some ancient family trees to understand that in medieval times many young women were forced into pregnancy in arranged marriages. Though there is record of Lady Macbeth having given birth, there is no record, I think, of the survival of a child. The facts, though, may help the actress to uncover the psychology of the lady. Had the too-young bride miscarried her first child? As a result, was the current Lady Macbeth no longer able to bear children?

Glossary

THEY the Weird Sisters.

WHILES while.

MISSIVES letters. (Actually, it is Ross who tells Macbeth of his new title, in Act 1, Scene 3. Here's a question. Could the use of the word "missive" be a stage direction for the earlier scene? Are we being told by the author that Ross also brought letters of entitlement to Macbeth in that earlier scene? (Just like an Agatha Christie, isn't it? Read James Thurber's *Macbeth Murder Mystery*!)

THE KING Duncan, the First. King of Scotland, reigned 1030-1040. Some historians maintain that Duncan was not the rightful king and that Macbeth, in fact, should have been crowned in his stead. This might be a point of view held by Lady Macbeth. Does this set the lady on a course of justifiable regicide?

THANE OF CAWDOR title given to Macbeth after being victorious in battle. I think this to be a bad omen, as the previous Cawdor was a traitor, but Lady Macbeth does not know this of Cawdor at this time.

WEIRD SISTERS same trio; "They" the three witches.

GLAMIS Pronounced Glahms as in Brahms. Macbeth's title before being granted the Thaneship of Cawdor. Glamis Castle is also the family home of Macbeth. The castle still exists.

HIE go quickly.

GOLDEN ROUND the crown of Scotland.

FERDINAND,
KING OF NAVARRE.

LOVE'S LABOUR'S LOST Act 1, Scene 1.
The park of Ferdinand, King of Navarre.
Ferdinand, Berowne, Longaville, and Dumaine

Ferdinand: Let fame, that all hunt after in their
lives,
Live regist'red upon our brazen tombs,
And then grace us in the disgrace of death;
When, spite of cormorant devouring Time,
Th' endeavour of this present breath may buy
That honour which shall bate his scythe's keen
edge,
And make us heirs of all eternity.
Therefore, brave conquerors, - for so you are
That war against your own affections
And the huge army of the world's desires -
Our late edict shall strongly stand in force:
Navarre shall be the wonder of the world,

Our court shall be a little academe,
Still and contemplative in living art.
You three, Berowne, Dumaine, and Longaville,
Have sworn for three years' term to live with me,
My fellow-scholars, and to keep those statutes
That are recorded in this schedule here.
Your oaths are passed; and now subscribe your
    names,
That his own hand may strike his honour down
That violates the smallest branch herein.
If you are armed to do, as sworn to do,
Subscribe to your deep oaths, and keep it too.

This is almost a prologue, in that this opening speech
sets up the plot of *Love's Labour's Lost*, but unlike the
Chorus in *Henry V*, here the premise is pronounced by one
of the leading characters within the play. Ferdinand, King
of Navarre, encourages his courtiers to sign a written contract, in extension of their previous oral agreement, which
could establish a new philosophical and social discipline
for the conduct of the king and his court.

The speech from the king of this province between
France and Spain has a certain declamatory aspect to it,
but with such things as "brave conquerors," "Navarre
shall be the wonder of the world," and "my fellow schol-
ars," Ferdinand exhibits a keen if restrained sense of
humor. There is a certain mystery here, too, about the
"schedule," the "oaths," and the invitation to sign on the
dotted line, which in turn sets up Longaville to agree,
Dumaine to agree, and last, Berowne to argue the point.
Being a well trained king, Ferdinand is comfortable with
pronouncements and it is possible there is some legitimate

comedy to be obtained even here at the outset. More comedy also, in this first speech of the play, from Ferdinand's use of the deed he wants to get signed. Clearly he has a natural authority with which he collects the mortified Dumaine and the altitudinal Longaville, and of which the sparkling Berowne is wary.

Ferdinand's opening lines are so over the top that one could imagine he has his tongue firmly rooted in his cheek. The idea that eschewing women for three years would win one a place in eternity is a bit rich, even for a devout king. That this game might be the means of somehow tempering the keen-edged scythe of Father Time is also very high-flown. We may sense that Ferdinand hopes that someone will have a shot at him. Mercifully, Berowne stops the adolescent contract dead in its tracks and the comedy is off and running. The chance is again here for the actor to set the tone for the evening. The speech has a majestic ring to it and not solely because it is spoken by a king. Silly ambition it is, for four grown men to aspire to such an agreement, and we know, or at least we hope, that the quartet will fall from their precarious perch as soon as the first woman hits the stage.

Which proves pretty well to be the case.

So, there is, I think, a certain jocular insecurity around this opening gambit of the king.

WHY: To establish the premise of forgoing the pleasures of women for three years. To introduce the four main men in the play, around whom the plot revolves. To draw Berowne into an argument in which he will speak against the new procedures?

WHERE: Don Armado's letter, read later in the scene, indicates that this first meeting is in the park adjacent to the home of the king of Navarre. It suits the unnatural premise of denying women to be surrounded by the very nature that would be denied. Apropos of location, here, as in many other places, Bill tells you where things are happening. One sometimes has to look elsewhere in the text, but usually such things are stated. In *As You Like It*, for example, Sylvius clearly states in his second scene with Corin a circumstance which must have taken place in his first scene with that character of the elderly shepherd, but which is not mentioned in that first scene. As I implied earlier, there is no substitute in the final analysis for reading the entire play.

WHO: There is no direct address of an audience here, as there was with the *Henry V* Chorus; no aside, as with the letter of Lady Macbeth. The only audience for Ferdinand is his three colleagues.

OTHER: What is established is the premise for the entire battle of the sexes that rages throughout the play and the hierarchy of Ferdinand's three friendly courtiers. Clearly one may not, without the use of heavy irony, cast a short actor in the role of Longaville. Just a thought. Is this another group of out-of-work soldiers, newly returned from a conflict, and who now don't have anything sensible to do with themselves but take up arms against their "own affections"? They are referred to as "brave conquerors."

Glossary

CORMORANT a greedy, diving waterbird.

BATE check, restrain, moderate.

HIS SCYTHE Father Time; of course, you knew.

NAVARRE small region of southwestern France. Here it is possible that the king is referring to himself as "the wonder of the world."

OUR COURT a good example of the royal we, or in this case, our.

ACADEME school, academy. Pronounced akadeem.

BEROWNE a courtier. Sometimes pronounced Brown.

DUMAINE another courtier. Does Dumaine overuse his hands? De main, in French, is "of the hand." Might be a joke.

LONGAVILLE a third and, we are told, taller courtier. The height of this character is a running gag through the play.

SCHEDULE another stage direction. He must be carrying something, or have something to which he may refer this line.

SUBSCRIBE same as for "schedule." Does Ferdinand have to carry pen and ink, or has he a scribe in tow? Is it a quill pen? Could it be a ball point? Laptop?

PROLOGUE

ROMEO AND JULIET
Enter Chorus

Chorus: Two households, both alike in dignity,
In fair Verona, where we lay our scene,
From ancient grudge break to new mutiny,
Where civil blood makes civil hands unclean.
From forth the fatal loins of these two foes
A pair of star-crossed lovers take their life
Whose misadventured piteous overthrows
Doth with their death bury their parents' strife.
The fearful passage of their death-marked love,
And the continuance of their parents' rage,
Which, but their children's end, nought could remove,
Is now the two hours' traffic of our stage;
The which if you with patient ears attend,
What here shall miss, our toil shall strive to mend.

Here is an effortless prologue of just fourteen lines, with which an actor should be able to demonstrate his or her ability and authority with verse. There is not a great requirement here for emotional eruption, but there is nevertheless something to master in the composure and analytical quality of this prologue.

This chorus is rightly distanced from the star-crossed lovers, and one feels that the speaker is somehow above it all, which may be why it is so often played from the character of the Prince of Verona. I think it should not however be the Prince, since the speaker is clearly demonstrating his position as an interlocutor. The Prince, being a part of the play, may not easily speak the prologue. A neutral chorus is better able to apologize, for instance, for the "two hours traffic of our stage" alluded to at the end of the speech.

Has there ever been a successful production of this play which took only two hours? Has there ever been a production which was so snappy? I rather doubt it. Certainly one should not be inclined to haste with this prologue, whatever the author implies about the overall length of the play.

WHY: To establish the plot and the story outline. It is a lesson followed by the late Alfred Hitchcock, to let the audience know something concerning plot and motivation that the characters in the play do not know. Hence we, the audience in the cinema, are rightly suspicious of Anthony Perkins' character at the Bates Motel, long before Janet Leigh's character need be. Here, in *Romeo and Juliet*, we are told outright that the now famous "star-crossed lovers" die before the end of the play. More, we are informed that they commit suicide. That blows any idea of suspense before the curtain has barely gone up, and we have to get on with appreciating the play on other levels.

WHERE: Again the prologue is spoken from the no-man's-land of somewhere between the fact of the audience being in the theatre and the characters of the play being in Verona. A choice for the actor and possibly, if there is still one around, a director.

WHO: Again, spoken only to the audience in the theatre. Although I imagine, in a pinch, this prologue could be dictated to a scribe. A reporter filing his story for the late news? It would have to be CNN for a two-hour newscast.

OTHER: It is a quite cold-blooded and succinct appraisal of what is about to happen. Indeed, the difficulty of the speech may be its very simplicity and directness. In my personal experience, "simplicity" and "directness" are two profoundly moving qualities, not always readily visible in performance, much less at an audition. Often the decision not to "act" is a great gift. One problem with conventional auditions is that the situation is usually so false, particularly in that there is no one to whom the auditioning actor may react. Too often, actors, particularly young actors, feel they must do too much. Remember, though, that the requirements of many auditions often leave very little room for "acting." It is always as well to think of an audition as requiring a quite different technique than normal work in a theatre, be it performing or rehearsal.

Glossary

VERONA a city in Northern Italy. Verona is at the
same latitude as Milan to the west and Venice to
the east; midway between the two. (See Renato
Castellini's film of *Romeo and Juliet*, in which the
late Laurence Harvey plays Romeo and much of
which is shot in Verona.)

HOUSEHOLDS not just family but the the entire retinue of the house and master. Hence the many fric-
tions in this play between servants of the two rival
families.

CIVIL BLOOD not an official war or dispute, but a
feud which is by no means "civil."

HENRY IV

HENRY IV, Part 1 Act 1, Scene 1.
London: The Palace
King Henry with Sir Walter Blunt, meeting
Westmoreland and others

Henry: So shaken as we are, so wan with care,
Find we a time for frighted peace to pant,
And breathe short-winded accents of new broils
To be commenced in strands afar remote:
No more the thirsty entrance of this soil
Shall daub her lips with her own children's blood,
No more shall trenching war channel her fields,
Nor bruise her flowerets with the armèd hoofs
Of hostile paces: those opposèd eyes,
Which like the meteors of a troubled heaven,
All of one nature, of one substance bred,
Did lately meet in the intestine shock
And furious close of civil butchery,

31

Shall now, in mutual well-beseeming ranks,
March all one way, and be no more opposed
Against acquaintance, kindred, and allies....
The edge of war, like an ill-sheathèd knife,
No more shall cut his master....Therefore, friends,
As far as to the sepulchre of Christ,
Whose soldier now, under whose blessèd cross
We are impressèd and engaged to fight,
Forthwith a power of English shall we levy,
Whose arms were moulded in their mothers' womb
To chase these pagans in those holy fields
Over whose acres walked those blesse`d feet
Which fourteen hundred years ago were nailed
For our advantage on the bitter cross....
But this our purpose now is twelve month old,
And bootless 'tis to tell you we will go:
Therefore we meet not now. Then let me hear
Of you, my gentle cousin Westmoreland,
What yesternight our council did decree
In forwarding this dear expedience.

Henry, who was Bolingbroke (*see Richard II*), and a
usurper of the throne of England, having, he thought, no
more wars to fight at home, decided to embark upon a crusade to the Holy Land. The first person he talks to tells him
that there is another campaign being fought and lost at
home against the Welsh. The suggested crusade to the Holy
Land promptly takes a back seat. I think that Henry IV the
man was riddled with guilt at the killing of Richard II,
through which Henry took the throne of England. He
thinks that he will be cleansed in some way by going to the
Holy Land on a crusade. We do know that a pilgrimage to

Jerusalem was a long held ambition, and one which Henry never realized. The closest this king got to the Holy Land was that he was taken ill in Westminster Abbey, with what is thought now to be a heart attack and he did in fact die in a side chamber of the Abbey, which the friars had long since nicknamed "Jerusalem."

This opening speech of *Henry IV, Part 1*, is a very rich and powerful plea for peace. It was a plea to no avail since the civil wars in this play raged on, as they did in historic England, for many years beyond the time depicted here.

There is an interesting use of the royal "we" in the opening lines and yet another example, with which Bill's writing is crammed, of a soldier who thinks he has no war to fight and therefore no function in life. Henry's solution to the supposed peace on the home front is to go off and bash the so-called infidel in the Middle East, rather similar to the first President Bush, really; having a go at Saddam Hussein, a year before election time. Very similar, too, to the Iron Maiden Margaret Thatcher creating a war in the Falklands in order to secure another general election in England in the early 1980s. Nothing changes! Watch the evening news. See *Wag the Dog*. Henry's invention of a crusade fits right in with the political syndrome discussed in that excellent movie.

I think the speech here is so weighed down with guilt and religious imagery that it may be given, at times, an almost chantlike tone. It is even possible that Henry is in the midst of some religious rite at the outset of the play. I once saw the highly respected New York actor, Bernard Kates, play this opening salvo in monastic robes, and with Mr. Kates fine delivery and the religious overtone to the speech, it worked very well indeed. I understand that such a line of action may not be everyone's choice, but it is a thought. Again, because this is the opening speech of the play, it is wide open to interpretation by the thinking actor.

WHY: This man was made king through open acts of aggression. Henry IV was not trained for kingship and perhaps he does not know how to rule without fighting a war. Hence the crusade and the hope of a common enemy for his barons and knights. We know too that there was vast wealth in precious metal to be collected in the Holy Land. Take a look at modern-day Venice and ask someone where those four gold horses in the Piazza San Marco really come from. Crusades were like a field exercise to keep the army together, and in my opinion they often had very little to do with religion. They carried with them the added bonus that the constant looting provided the western European soldiers and the kings in charge with much money in the long run. Much as it is today with many military leaders, drug running and the profits therefrom are similar to the four gold horses of yesteryear. No doubt Bill would have written a good play about Oliver North and Irangate.

WHERE: Probably an anteroom in a private chapel, or in an abbey within the city of London. Henry, I think, became rather over-religious after deposing Richard and probably spent a great deal of his reign on his middle-aged knees. Is the speech perhaps almost a prayer in the first part and a sermon in the second?

WHO: Henry could be speaking either to his God, or his court, or both. It is not a speech principally directed at the audience in the theatre, but, like Navarre's opening salvo in *Love's Labour's Lost*, it comes close.

OTHER: The intention here is to set a scene. The recently established peace and the potential crusade are the leading items in Henry's news bulletin. The speech outlines quickly the life that was. What will now happen on the day that is? I see it as very much wishful thinking on Henry's part that his troubles at home are over. As the play goes on to demonstrate, Henry's court is virtually riddled with malcontents and upstart lords and earls, many thinking that they might, in time, usurp the usurper. The king may well be "shaken" and "wan," since the business of government is tiring and fatigue is not usually alleviated by excessive guilt. Certainly, Henry could not manage the country any longer by himself; in fairly short order he is forced to recruit the services of his soon-to-prove-brilliant son, who would later become Henry V, one of the greatest military leaders in English history. Not a bad king either, Henry V, but one who died young.

It may be interesting to think of Henry IV as a tired man trying to be strong. The dilemma of the recently unemployed soldier, as I say, is one of Bill's constant themes: Benedick, Coriolanus, Falstaff, Henry V, Macbeth, Richard III, Titus, and many others.

Glossary

STRANDS beaches.
INTESTINE internal, civil.
CIVIL BUTCHERY civil war.
SEPULCHRE OF CHRIST Jerusalem.
PAGANS truly, anyone at this time who did not conform to the Church of Rome. Henry IV, consider-

ing himself a good Catholic, would have considered the Welsh to be just as much pagans as those
inhabitants of the Middle East to whom he here
refers.

BLESSED FEET you know, those feet that were thought
to have been nailed to a cross at Calvary.

BOOTLESS without point, redundant.

YESTERNIGHT interesting that the Privy Council is
already working nights.

"A PASSION TO TATTERS"

The following are some speeches wherein it is, in my opinion, all too easy to allow your anger, anguish, torment, or spleen to run away with the text. These speeches require such jockeyship as you might give a thoroughbred horse on a tight track. Do not let these speeches get the bit between their teeth lest you lose your saddle and take a serious tumble.

MARULLUS

JULIUS CAESAR Act 1, Scene 1.
Rome, a street.
Flavius, Marullus, and certain Commoners

Marullus Wherefore rejoice? What conquest brings
   he home?
What tributaries follow him to Rome,
To grace in captive bonds his chariot-wheels?
You blocks, you stones, you worse than senseless
   things!
O you hard hearts, you cruel men of Rome,
Knew you not Pompey? Many a time and oft
Have you climbed up to walls and battlements,
To towers and windows, yea, to chimney-tops,
Your infants in your arms, and there have sat
The live-long day with patient expectation
To see great Pompey pass the streets of Rome:

And when you saw his chariot but appear,
Have you not made an universal shout,
That Tiber trembled underneath her banks
To hear the replication of your sounds
Made in her concave shores?
And do you now put on your best attire?
And do you now cull out a holiday?
And do you now strew flowers in his way
That comes in triumph over Pompey's blood?
Be gone!
Run to your houses, fall upon your knees,
Pray to the gods to intermit the plague
That needs must light on this ingratitude.

This is a most appropriate speech with which to begin
this section of potentially overwrought passions.

Marullus is so angry that it must become clear to all
attendant that he may not long survive in this new Rome
of Caesar. In fact, in this play Marullus does not last as
long as Caesar himself. A mere scene or two after this early
speech, the tribune is reported killed.

Marullus is outraged that the people in the streets, the
artisans, should have so quickly forgotten the man,
Pompey, who was so recently in their good graces. A
Kennedy supporter perhaps, shortly after Johnson came so
suddenly to power, although the circumstances of that
changeover appear to be just a little different: long range
bullets for JFK as opposed to short range knives for JC.
The intricacies of "conspiracy" surrounding both assassi-
nations may be much the same.

This high level of anger coming from Marullus may be

extremely difficult to contain for the actor. Hence Bill's note to the players at Elsinore about not attempting to "tear a passion to tatters" should be well heeded. It must be a livid anger, I think, but it must have some sense of cohesion, which will get the actor to the end of the speech and the character virtually and for me regrettably to the end of his life. As I said, the death of Marullus with anger presumably unabated, is reported very soon after he makes the speech. The people around Caesar were not going to tolerate a counter-revolution quite so soon after the great leader's succession, or so they thought.

The anger of the tribune Marullus here may be contrasted with the cold-bloodedness of the upper echelon assassins, who failed to talk Caesar to death politically and who are shortly hereafter finally reduced to knifing the emperor of Rome in the very Senate itself.

WHY: Simply because Marullus was devoted to the Rome of Pompey, and probably in addition devoted to the individual, Pompey. In his capacity as a tribune, Marullus would be provided with ample opportunity to understand both the political strategy and the military force and expertise of the great Pompey. Marullus seems genuinely surprised that the city of Rome is in such a festive mood so soon after the death of Pompey, someone Marullus considered to be a remarkable leader, and one who was, let's face it, a former peer of Julius Caesar.

WHERE: Any street or public place in Rome. In reference to environment, it may be interesting, architecturally, that ancient Rome was not noted for its "towers and windows," or for its "battlements," and certainly not in those days for its "chimney-tops." As he often does, here the author is expertly making points of reference that his audience in England will more readily understand.

WHO: The man in the street is the target for the speech. By extension, Bill is appealing to his audience with another facet of one of his constant themes, which was that we should always preserve the status quo. The writer was frequently defending the state, irrespective, sometimes, of what the state was up to politically. The Romans, who are carving out their holiday without the slightest recognition of why they are having such a holiday, can be seen as guild members in the City of London, or as revelers at a rally in Nuremberg in the 1930's. Rather mindless. In fact, it is most likely in the Rome of the day the holiday was an extension of an existing holiday or feast day. Spring was a busy time of the year for the Roman gods. We know it is spring, don't we? As we know that Caesar was assasinated around the Ides of March, the middle of the month.

OTHER: Marullus hopes to achieve a complete turn around of the situation. Fired up by his own rhetoric, he is off to post flyers bearing his views and to tear down any opposing statements. The speech here and the anger of it are his undoing. The character of Marullus, as depicted here, does almost tear a passion to tatters, and it certainly seems that in his high state of passionate feeling concerning Pompey, and thoughtless of his own welfare, he tears his life apart. Beware! The actor who plays Marullus must not become too impassioned. This is a speech in which the actor must learn something about containing great anger, and then put the learning to good use.

Incidentally this is a rather good speech for checking your breathing. It is so difficult to contain emotionally, and quite difficult to breathe at times, that you may find it, once absorbed, to be a very useful exercise with which to examine your lungpower. I used to know that if I couldn't breathe this speech, I was not ready to act in a theatre.

Apropos of those battlements and chimney tops: There is much talked and written about Bertolt Brecht's creating a style of "alienation," but here it is, right here; this Elizabethan author of great genius constantly reminded his audience that they were watching a play. Remember too that the actors playing the original production of *Julius Caesar* would have played it in doublet and hose, not in togas. You should play the speech however you feel, but perhaps not in doublet and hose at an audition.

Glossary

CAPTIVE BONDS Common practice to tether newly captured slaves to the wheels of the returning chariots when parading into the city.

POMPEY Roman general, statesman, and member of the First Triumvirate. Pronounced Pompee (and not to be confused with Pompeii, the city near Vesuvius which was buried beneath an avalanche of molten lava and ash in 79 AD and which is pronounced Pompay.) Pompey obtained refuge in Egypt and was killed there. Timescale once more. Pompey died, we think, four years or so before Caesar. Dramatic license allows us to imagine that Marullus's wounds are still fresh. At least we may imagine that the tribune was devoted to his former general. As well he might have been, for by most accounts Pompey was a military leader of some genius.

TIBER the river of Rome.

RUN TO YOUR HOUSES The people of Rome had many religious shrines in their homes.

PRINCE HAL

HENRY IV Part 1 Act 3, Scene 2.
A palace.
Prince Hal

Prince Hal: Do not think so. You shall not find
    it so;
And God forgive them that so much have swayed
Your majesty's good thoughts away from me!
I will redeem all this on Percy's head,
And in the closing of some glorious day
Be bold to tell you that I am your son,
When I will wear a garment all of blood,
And stain my favors in a bloody mask,
Which, wash'd away, shall scour my shame with it.
And that shall be the day, whene'er it lights,
That this same child of honour and renown,
This gallant Hotspur, this all-praisèd knight,

And your unthought-of Harry chance to meet.
For every honour sitting on his helm,
Would they were multitudes, and on my head
My shames redoubled! for the time will come,
That I shall make this northern youth exchange
His glorious deeds for my indignities.
Percy is but my factor, good my lord,
To engross up glorious deeds on my behalf,
And I will call him to so strict account
That he shall render every glory up,
Yea, even the slightest worship of his time,
Or I will tear the reckoning from his heart....
This, in the name of God I promise here,
The which if He be pleased I shall perform,
I do beseech your majesty may salve
The long-grown wounds of my intemperature:
If not, the end of life cancels all bands,
And I will die a hundred thousand deaths
Ere break the smallest parcel of this vow.

One of the greatest father and son scenes in English
dramatic literature, this encounter gives the actor playing
Hal, the Prince of Wales and heir to the throne of England,
a wonderfully well-rounded opportunity to portray contained rage, or outrage.

Hal is irate here at his father's accusations concerning
Hal's recent public behavior, and the estranged son may be
the more irate because he must know that there is at least
some foundation for the rumors that have reached his
father's court.

It might be useful to know that this was not an acciden-
tal interview. We do know that Hal was summoned by the

king, his father, and that Hal was given enough notice of the conference to enable him to have a special tunic tailored, which he wore on the occasion of this reconciliation with Henry IV, his father. I mention this because in the scene itself, great patience is required on the part of the Prince of Wales. The longer the time Hal is kept waiting before he can properly state his point of view, the more pent up his anger and, paradoxically, his love for his father may become. When Hal finally erupts with "Do not think so..." it might be a volcano blowing its top.

Hal's speech, with its powerful undertow, can be seen almost as a religious affirmation. Indeed the speech begins with an oath and ends with one, "And God forgive..." and "I will die a hundred thousand deaths."

For the first time we see Hal's true majesty powerful, smooth. The specially made tunic could indicate that the prince was prepared for the interview; and more to the point, if you wish, that he was "acting." Remember, this was the man who would soon become Henry V, often depicted by Bill as a role player. Read *Henry V*.

Incidentally, and in my opinion it is a huge, theatrical incidental - the actual Prince of Wales chose for this interview to be dressed in a powder-blue satin tunic, slashed across the bodice and sleeves. The vertical slashes were individually bound, like buttonholes. The needles used for the binding were left hanging in each cut, suspended by the sewing thread. Punk? By the standards of Hal's life and times, that was a daring and provocative fashion statement, which might seem to contradict his passionate promissory note to his overreligious father. I don't think so. I think it more likely that Hal had this garment so tailored in order to give himself a "costume" within which to perform his new role as the savior of the country. He was indeed not only the savior of his father but the savior of England for much of his short life. It must have been a huge piece of theatre, the actual interview, when one thinks of this young man dressed in such a manner and still able to persuade his father to take him back into the fold. Looks may sometimes deceive.

WHY: The country is facing civil war and the king, Henry IV, has summoned his son, Prince Henry (Hal) to ask for his assistance. Hal, desperate to be asked and overjoyed that he was, attends in order to establish a new identity for himself in his father's court.

WHERE: An anteroom in the palace of Westminster, probably. Westminster at that time was the twin city to London and only a few minutes from the City of London. Today Westminster is completely surrounded by Greater London.

WHO: It must be the choice of the actor as to how many others are in attendance at the beginning, but the king dismisses people early on and the father and son confront each other alone for the greater part of the scene. Hal is in his early twenties, his father, in his mid-forties.

OTHER: The play is entirely regenerated through the union created at the end of this scene. The two previously disparate forces of Hal and his father are brought together and a civil war is brought to a successful, if temporary, conclusion.

Every Prince of Wales since Hal, who became the role model, has had the same problem in England; namely that of not being properly employed during the reign of the parents. Prince Charles, the current Prince of Wales, has exactly the same problems as those of Hal, mostly caused by the frustration at being kept waiting in the wings and not being given a sensible role to play in current affairs. No doubt Prince Charles has to play this scene with his mother Queen Elizabeth II. If so, I hope he speaks with as much eloquence as Bill attributes here to Hal.

A thought about Hotspur, and Hal's attitude toward him. As Hal talks about Hotspur in this speech, you might want to consider that it is widely accepted that Hotspur had some form of speech impediment. There are contemporary ballads and broadsheets commenting on the speech of Harry Percy, Hotspur. It is for the actor playing Percy to determine in a production what the manner was of Percy's "thickness of speech," but here and for the purposes of an audition the actor playing Hal may give Hotspur any reasonable impediment he wishes. Might Hal play with a stammer on the H of "Hotspur" or the k of "knight?" Just a thought. I did not see Laurence Olivier as Hal, but I believe that when Olivier's Hal killed Hotspur at the end of the play (Act 5, Scene 4), Olivier took the word "worms" out of his Hotspur's mouth and stammered on the beginning of his own line, "For worms, brave Percy, fair thee well, great heart." Making the line: "For w-w-w-orms, brave P-P-P-Percy, fair thee w-w-well, great heart." Not a stroke of genius, but an interesting thought worth exploring.

Again, sometimes a most important clue to the playing of a character may appear buried in the back end of a play. The probability is that an actor such as Olivier (not that there have been any) might have discovered the opportunity in rehearsal and realigned the whole part to accommodate his discovery. Such a truly generous man as Olivier would only have done so with the support and agreement of the actor playing Hotspur to his Hal. Once more, read the whole play.

Glossary

PERCY Sir Henry Percy (1366-1403), otherwise known as Hotspur.

HELM helmet.

NORTHERN YOUTH Hotspur or Percy. Officially, Sir Henry Percy, son of the 1st Earl of Northumberland, a region of Northern England.

GLORIOUS DEEDS Hotspur, unlike Hal, had many battle honors at this time, and had distinguished himself many times in battles against the Scots.

FACTOR steward or servant.

ENGROSS monopolize.

SALVE balm, or to apply balm.

ROMEO

ROMEO AND JULIET Act 3, Scene 3.
Friar Lawrence's cell.

Romeo

Romeo: 'Tis torture and not mercy. Heaven is here
Where Juliet lives, and every cat and dog
And little mouse, every unworthy thing,
Live here in Heaven and may look on her,
But Romeo may not. More validity,
More honourable state, more courtship, lives
In carrion flies than Romeo: they may seize
On the white wonder of dear Juliet's hand
And steal immortal blessing from her lips,
Who even in pure and vestal modesty
Still blush, as thinking their own kisses sin;
But Romeo may not - he is banishèd.
Flies may do this, but I from this must fly:
They are free men but I am banishèd.

And say'st thou yet that exile is not death?
Hadst thou no poison mixed, no sharp-ground
    knife,
No sudden mean of death, though ne'er so mean,
But "banishèd" to kill me? "Banishèd!"
O Friar, the damnèd use that word in hell,
Howling attends it. How hast thou the heart,
Being a divine, a ghostly confessor,
A sin-absolver and my friend professed,
To mangle me with that word "banishèd?"

Hiding in Friar Lawrence's cell, Romeo receives news
from the friar that the Prince of Verona has not exacted the
full penalty for the street murder of Tybalt by Romeo. The
prince has not issued the death penalty, which the law
allows. "Not body's death, but body's banishment," that's
the sentence. The friar thinks the news is good, but everything is relative and Romeo focuses on the banishment and
varies his theme to make the prince's sentence many
degrees more punishing than mere death.

The friar tells Romeo that the sentence is dear mercy.
The use of the word "mercy" sets the young lover off on a
frenzied, angry description of his plight as he sees it.
Placing himself in a region somewhere below dogs and
cats, working his comparison down to that of a common
fly, and eventually turning on the troubled priest, Romeo
provides here a wonderful opportunity in which to resist
tearing a passion to tatters.

Romeo must be understood here, and only by tempering
his despair can he (and the actor) survive. It is the nadir of
Romeo's life to date. Romeo must be in a state of great

mental anguish but he and the actor playing Romeo must be understood; Romeo is angry with the prince, but he must obey the sentence; he is alienating the friar, but he is in the friar's cell and totally beholden to him. Many checks and balances. Throughout his pain, his anger, and his aggression, Romeo (and the actor) must keep the words of this complex speech going forward.

"Flies may do this but I from this must fly." A sense of humor, or wit, at least, energizes the depths of Romeo's anguish.

WHY: It is a fine example of how we can lose our sense of perspective, see black for white and white for black. The frustration of youth; the ineptness of religious leadership; the drowning man clutching at a straw.

WHERE: The rooms of Friar Lawrence somewhere within the city walls of Verona. The friar seems to live alone, and we know that he is a herbalist of some distinction, though his science serves no one any good in this tragedy. The room could almost be a laboratory.

WHO: The friar is very much a father figure for Romeo and one who the youth thinks can be called upon in times of trouble. As it is, the friar, I think, makes a huge mistake with the lives of this young couple.

OTHER: Romeo is very much a spent force after this scene. He has always been a little headstrong, to say the least, but in blowing his top so gratuitously here, he seems to lose all sense of proportion and is clearly destined for tragic consequences. He cannot bear life any longer.

Glossary

HEAVEN IS HERE In Verona? In some part of Romeo's anatomy? Probably the former.

BANISHÈD Just to remind the reader here that the editor, Dover Wilson, in this case, uses "èd" to denote the stress. He uses a straightforward "ed," without an accent, when he thinks there is no such stress. The stressed "èd" at the end of this "banishèd" pays huge dividends, with so much, almost grinding repetition of the word.

MEAN OF DEATH means of death.

NE'ER SO MEAN be it ever so small.

GHOSTLY CONFESSOR Usually, the priest hearing the confession is unseen by the one making the confession.

SHYLOCK

THE MERCHANT OF VENICE Act 1, Scene 3.
A street in Venice.
Shylock, Bassanio, Antonio

Shylock: Signor Antonio, many a time and oft
In the Rialto you have rated me
About my moneys and my usances:
Still have I borne it with a patient shrug,
For suff'rance is the badge of all our tribe.
You call me misbeliever, cut-throat dog,
And spit upon my Jewish gaberdine,
And all for use of that which is mine own.
Well then, it now appears you need my help:
Go to then; you come to me, and you say,
"Shylock, we would have moneys:" you say so!
You, that did void your rheum upon my beard,
And foot me as you spurn a stranger cur

Over your threshold. Moneys is your suit.
What should I say to you? Should I not say
"Hath a dog money? is it possible
A cur can lend three thousand ducats?" or
Shall I bend low, and in a bondman's key,
With bated breath, and whisp'ring humbleness,
Say this:
"Fair sir, you spit on me on Wednesday last-
You spurn'd me such a day-another time
You called me dog; and for these courtesies
I'll lend you thus much moneys?"

Witty, urbane, taunting, intelligent, patient, tolerant,
imaginative, strong, ingenuous,and maybe most surpris-
ingly, generous. Is that Shylock? It is here, before the
abduction of his only daughter, before the burglary of his
house, before the theft of his jewelry, servants, collateral,
and heirlooms. Here, before the disruption of his entire
household by the so-called Christians in the play, Shylock
appears to have been a most reasonable man.

Keep in mind that Shylock is antipathetic to Christians,
perhaps not on religious grounds, but because the
Christian moneylenders worked their way through the
Venice of his day, seemingly taking interest in kind only,
and thereby forgoing the directness of and perhaps avoid-
ing the stigma attached to mere monetary interest.
However they wished to appear, many Christians were
merchants and moneylenders, as was Shylock. It is the pre-
tension on the part of some Christians, I think, that distin-
guishes them from Shylock.

Here, in the street going about his business, he appears
to me to be light, witty, and tantalized in his reception of

the request to lend three thousand ducats to the Christian Antonio.

Admittedly, we see from the preamble to the speech that Shylock could not resist keeping Antonio and company waiting as he gives a light dissertation on Jacob's sheep. There is no doubt, you have to edge your way around, "How like a fawning publican he looks. I hate him for he is a Christian." For what it is worth, if I were directing this play I would lean strongly on the above-mentioned Christian attitude of not appearing to take monetary interest for monetary loans as the real bone of contention.

Most important, Shylock is not a stupid man and the deal he eventually suggests, of a pound of flesh, need not be seen as malice aforethought. Shylock, of all people, would know that no court in the land, or even in the known world, would be likely to uphold such a bond. Later in the play, and driven mad by the appalling abduction of his only daughter and the previously mentioned and various criminal activities, all of which were conducted by close friends of Antonio against Shylock's estate or person, Shylock eventually does seek recourse in the law. Much good it does him. That last- minute pursuit of the law is an action of a man who has been unquestionably abused by the very people to whom he loaned a substantial sum of money gratis.

WHY: Big scene setting up many premises for the remainder of the play. The life that might have been, rather than the life in which Antonio and Bassanio soon involve themselves and Shylock. What if Shylock had simply said "I am so sorry, I have a slight cash flow problem myself." Very short play. Might Shylock be thinking at some time to say such a thing?

WHERE: A street, or canalside, in Venice, probably middle morning. The Rialto was the Wall Street of Venice, if you like.

WHO: Quite probable that Shylock and Antonio had done business before. It is the abhorrent behavior of Bassanio, and his money grabbing ego, that comes between the two merchants here. The sycophantic Bassanio, with Gratiano maybe looking out for him, possibly with Lorenzo along for the laughs, would give Shylock a small audience which he may play off while talking to Antonio. It may well be only Bassanio and Antonio.

OTHER: If Shylock was a successful moneylender, and he was, he must have an air about him that is acceptable to the society to whom he will lend money. He should not be portrayed, as he often is, as some sullen Fagin-like character skulking around in the shadows. He has a respected and proper place in the Venetian society of his day, as did many Jews.

Glossary

RIALTO Wall Street, for all intents and purposes.
RATED ME berated me.
USANCES benefits of ownership.
RHEUM mucus, such as might develop with a cold or the flu.
BATED BREATH restrained breath, soft tones.
BONDSMAN'S KEY servant's tone of voice.

HASTINGS

RICHARD III Act 3, Scene 4.
The Tower of London.
Hastings, Ratcliffe, Lovel

Hastings: Woe, woe, for England! Not a whit
    for me;
For I, too fond, might have prevented this.
Stanley did dream the boar did raze our helms,
And I did scorn it, and disdain to fly:
Three times to-day my foot-cloth horse did stumble,
And started when he looked upon the Tower,
As loath to bear me to the slaughter-house.
O now I need the priest that spake to me:
I now repent I told the pursuivant,
As too triumphing, how mine enemies
To-day at Pomfret bloodily were butchered
And I myself secure in grace and favour.
O Margaret, Margaret, now thy heavy curse

Is lighted on poor Hastings' wretched head!
(Ratcliffe: Come, come, dispatch; the duke would
    be at dinner:
Make a short shrift, he longs to see your head.)
O momentary grace of mortal men,
Which we more hunt for than the grace of God!
Who builds his hope in air of your good looks
Lives like a drunken sailor on a mast,
Ready with every nod to tumble down
Into the fatal bowels of the deep.
(Lovel: Come, come, dispatch; 'tis bootless to ex-
    claim.)
O bloody Richard! miserable England!
I prophesy the fearfull'st time to thee
That ever wretched age hath looked upon.
Come, lead me to the block, bear him my head.
They smile at me who shortly shall be dead.

NB: Delete bracketed lines for audition.

I have included this departure speech because it provides
the auditioning actor with a good opportunity to demonstrate a wonderful dying fall.

The man, Lord Hastings, is in quick succession, surprised, out-maneuvered, defeated, and sentenced to death.
There is no way out and Hastings knows it. The speech is
a great example of regret and ruefulness, tinged with a
sense of humor even in the last seconds of his life. Not at
all declamatory, as it is sometimes performed, but simple,
poetic, and worldly-wise. Mentally, and maybe literally,
snapping his fingers, while saying, as most of us do every
day, "I should have known better." The difference from the

everyday here is that this is a matter of life and death. A
classic case of a man being in the wrong place at the wrong
time. Hastings would be the first to appreciate that
Richard could take him out sooner or later; it was only
ever a matter of time and of timing. Hastings has watched
this sort of thing happen to others and he is certainly no
innocent.

This speech is, I think, a wonderful example of the so-
called stiff upper lip of the English aristocracy. It does
indeed take some composure when faced with death to
simply comment that you knew when your horse missed its
footing in the early morning that this was not going to be
a good day. It is worthy of Clint Eastwood in some of his
finer moments and it is called understatement. An invalu-
able tool for the good actor. No passion in tatters here,
please.

WHY: It is the end of Hastings in the play, of course, and
a warning to everyone in the court that if this can happen
to him and so quickly (while the council are waiting for a
bowl of strawberries to be delivered) then it can happen to
anyone. This speech is but a lull before the next storm.
Cyclone Richard is about to come howling through.

WHERE: A room in the Tower of London, which is on the
north side of the River Thames. The Tower was not merely a prison at this time, but had many houses, state rooms,
and other quarters, some of which were customarily used
for Privy Council business. A good place, in this instance,
for a planning meeting about the forthcoming coronation.
Good for Richard at least, but not so good for Hastings. As
always, the Tower was a great place in which to dispatch
an enemy, and here Richard makes full use of the facility to

dispose of Lord Hastings. There was probably a beheading block in the center courtyard, as there still is today. At least Hastings did not have far to walk to his execution.

WHO: Seconds before Hastings has been with his peers of the Privy Council in a quite placid meeting about the stage-managing of royal events in London. He makes a fatal, for him, slip of the tongue and is soon dispatched by a couple of Richard, Duke of Gloucester's henchmen.

OTHER: There is a certain lyrical quality about the speech, which if properly exploited gives Hastings a fine exit from the play. (I know, Hastings has a small scene as a ghost before the final battle in Act 5.)

"Woe, woe, for England...." may be the ultimate in not tearing a passion to tatters, in that Hastings is able to think despite the confusion of hearing his death sentence and is able to voice an eloquently stated point of view about himself and the welfare of his country. Interesting, perhaps, that the very sophisticated Hastings is still subject to thoughts of omens, oaths, and curses. Are religion and the civilized world falling away as Richard goes into his final rampage? Hastings seems to know in his resignation that there is now no way to stop Richard. No way for Hastings, at least. It will take the gods, the totally unforeseen lack of a horse on the battlefield of Bosworth, and the betrayal of Lord Stanley in defecting with half of the king's army before Richard will finally be brought down. The last Plantagenet king.

One cannot lever too much history into any part of this play, but one should not leave *Richard III* without recommending Josephine Tey's remarkable book on the subject,

The Daughter of Time. It really is a detective story, and a very good one.

Glossary

STANLEY Lord Stanley, who ultimately betrayed Richard.

THE BOAR Richard's family emblem was a wild boar.

HELM armored headdress.

FOOT-CLOTH HORSE It must be winter. Hastings horse's hooves have been wrapped with canvas to prevent slipping and sliding.

THE TOWER Yes, of London.

PRIEST THAT SPAKE Hastings had earlier in the day acknowledged a priest in the street. That exchange is in Act 3, Scene 2.

PURSIEVANT herald.

POMFRET town in West Yorkshire, Northern England. Otherwise known as Pontefract, in whose castle the murder of Richard II took place in 1400. Hastings is making reference to the fact that several members of the royal family have recently taken refuge there and lost their lives as a consequence. Rivers, Grey, and Vaughan should really have known better, as Pomfret Castle must have been a stronghold of Richard III. Maybe that is the point; Hastings should also have known better than to ignore all the omens of the day.

MARGARET former queen of England, who had cursed Hastings.

THEY SMILE AT ME stage direction to the other actors involved in his arrest.

LADY ANNE

RICHARD III Act 1, Scene 2.
A street.
Enter the corpse of Henry VI, with halberdiers to guard it, Lady Anne *being the mourner attended by Tressel and Berkely*

Lady Anne: Set down, set down your honourable
    load—
If honour may be shrouded in a hearse—
Whilst I awhile obsequiously lament
Th' untimely fall of virtuous Lancaster.
Poor key-cold figure of a holy king!
Pale ashes of the house of Lancaster!
Thou bloodless remnant of that royal blood!
Be it lawful that I invocate thy ghost,
To hear the lamentations of poor Anne,
Wife to thy Edward, to thy slaught'red son,

Stabbed by the self same hand that made these
    wounds!
Lo, in these windows that let forth thy life,
I pour the helpless balm of my poor eyes.
O cursèd be the hand that made these holes!
Cursèd the blood that let this blood from hence!
Cursèd the heart that had the heart to do it!
 More direful hap betide that hated wretch,
That makes us wretched by the death of thee
Than I can wish to wolves - to spiders, toads,
Or any creeping venomed thing that lives!
If ever he have child, abortive be it,
Prodigious, and untimely brought to light,
Whose ugly and unnatural aspect
May fright the hopeful mother at the view;
And that be heir to his unhappiness!
If ever he have wife, let her be made
More miserable by the life of him
Than I am by my young lord's death and thee!
Come, now towards Chertsey with your holy load,
Taken from Paul's to be interrèd there;
And still, as you are weary of this weight,
Rest you, whiles I lament King Henry's corpse.

What a brilliant piece of staging by Bill here. He opens
his play with a bold soliloquy from his principal character,
and there ensues a lively scene involving manners, brother-
ly love, and skullduggerous behavior, at the end of which
Gloucester (Richard III) introduces the thought of his
intention to pursue Lady Anne, whose husband and father-
in-law he has recently killed in battle. In so doing, Richard

sets up Lady Anne's character in a few tantalizing lines of confession and fancy.

The opening of the play is all snap, crackle, and pop, and the entrance of Lady Anne, in widow's weeds and following her late father-in-law's coffin, is in great contrast.

Some interesting problems to solve here. Lady Anne is in mourning, and as a consequence, she is probably in a very depressed and submissive state of mind. Even her first line is as dolorous as a tolling bell. "Set down, set down, your honourable load." Immediately, though, we hear her intelligence when she picks up on the penultimate word: "If honor may be shrouded in a hearse." Throughout the lamentation there is a hatred of the perpetrator of her father-in-law's death, Richard of Gloucester, soon to be Richard III. There is strength in the hatred, but between the lamentation and the loathing we see a woman who appears to be almost totally off balance.

Without realizing it, in cursing Gloucester's future wife Lady Anne prophetically curses herself. She will, of course, marry Richard.

Anne's is the first real voice in the play which speaks against Richard, but she is upended and thrown further off balance by the ensuing scene of courtship, between her and, as she believes, the murderer of her husband and her father-in-law.

I think it is most significant that Lady Anne is on the way to an abbey with the corpse of a dead king. She is in a devoutly religious state of mind, and, paradoxically, because she is so steeped in the religion of the moment, she leaves herself entirely vulnerable to the "devil," which for her only seconds later in this scene, is Richard of Gloucester. Had Anne been in Richard's very real world instead of in a twilight zone of religious grief, she might well have been able to resist the temptations in the seduction scene. As it transpires, she is utterly outgunned by a man who plays on the very fact that she is at this moment so devout and so confused.

Richard is right, and it is a huge stage direction for the actor playing Lady Anne, when he later says, "Was ever woman in this manner wooed, was ever woman in this manner won?" By far it is Richard's (and Bill's) most audacious move in the play.

It is of some interest to me that two most audacious actors who have filmed the scene, (Ian McKellen and Laurence Olivier), both abridged and split the text, presumably because the outcome seems so improbable. For me the thing that makes it possible for Lady Anne to capitulate is the very improbability of her submitting under these circumstances, and that the poor soul is allowed absolutely no time to regain her bearings.

She is swept away rapidly, and for me it is the speed of Richard's attack here and not only the Lady's religious demeanor which is critical to her capitulation. In this play there is no earthly sanctuary from Richard when his blood is up. He is awe-inspiring. Indeed, another actor with more than a little audacity, Al Pacino, when he played the part on Broadway some years ago, had his audience literally clamoring for the next kill. Quite a sensational Richard III was Mr. Pacino. Do see Pacino's film on the subject, *Looking for Richard*. (In no way, for me, does the film give more than a glimpse of Pacino's riveting acting when he played the part, years before, at the Cort Theatre, but it is certainly worth researching. Not least for the views of the wonderfully articulate man in the street who is interviewed about the relevance of Shakespeare in our lives.)

I may seem to have strayed here in talking about

Richard rather than Lady Anne, but the point is that this monologue has to set up and feed into the great scene between the two characters. It is Anne's absolute preoccupation with the corpse before her which leaves her open to the oncoming assault.

This is a difficult speech to make "happen," but of course it has to just happen.

There is no scintilla of preparation for Lady Anne here, beyond the fact that with such journeys, the mourning party would customarily stop at a shrine or church gate and pray for the deceased. Here, Anne's intention in stopping seems mostly to originate in a feeling of charity for the poor men who are carrying the coffin. The rest of the speech....just happens.

WHY: Something of a situation report here, reminding us of Lancaster, kings, husbands; but the true point of the speech is to demonstrate how solid is Lady Anne's attitude, not to mention her venom, against Richard III. If Lady Anne capitulates here, if her resolution can be broken, then anything is possible for the remainder of the play.

WHERE: Somewhere between the City of London and Chertsey Abbey, which is some twenty miles to the southwest of London. A long walk if one is following a coffin; a longer walk still if one is carrying a coffin. It is likely, though, that this situation develops while the cortege is still in either London or Westminster. Richard, after Anne's exit but in this scene, redirects the corpse to Whitefriars, a district still in central London. He has no intention of trekking down to Chertsey with a dead body. Richard curiously invokes Saint Paul in the beginning of his scene with

Lady Anne, which might indicate that he was in the vicinity of the cathedral bearing that name, but it need not do so.

WHO: Initially, Lady Anne has a small group of people with her, most of whom are frightened off by Richard. It then becomes a one-on-one duel for which the lady is almost totally unprepared and, as it happens, ill-equipped. At the time of this monologue Anne's attendants could be scattered around her while she laments.

OTHER: It seems to me that one of the most difficult things to capture here is the fatigue of grief, while still sustaining the speech. Lady Anne must be exhausted. Her husband, her father- in-law, her position in life and in the court, all lost within a matter of weeks. In her despair she forgets the Christian ethic of praying for one's enemies. In fact, Anne is guilty here of invoking almost a black prayer, involving incantations of toads and reptiles, while in the middle of the deeply religious obligation of Burial of the Dead. Her black prayer is answered when she later marries Richard, and when she finds her spleen heaped upon herself.

Glossary

A HOLY KING Henry VI.

LANCASTER family opposed to York in the Wars of the Roses. Red rose for Lancaster, white rose for Yorkshire.

EDWARD heir to the throne of his father (Henry VI)

and the late husband of Lady Anne. Son (Edward) and father were both killed in battle by "Dick the Turd" (Richard III).

WINDOWS stab wounds on the corpse. Apparently still with blood on or around them.

HAP happenings.

PAUL'S St. Paul's Cathedral. The old wooden building, which later burned in the Great Fire of London; not the current, domed St. Paul's of Christopher Wren.

QUEEN MARGARET

HENRY VI Part 3 Act 1, Scene 1.
London: Parliament House.
Queen Margaret

Queen Margaret: Enforced thee! art thou king, and
    wilt be forced?
I shame to hear thee speak. Ah, timorous wretch!
Thou hast undone thyself, thy son, and me;
And given unto the house of York such head
As thou shalt reign but by their sufferance.
To entail him and his heirs unto the crown,
What is it, but to make thy sepulchre,
And creep into it far before thy time?
Warwick is chancellor and the lord of Calais;
Stern Faulconbridge commands the Narrow Seas;
The duke is made Protector of the realm;
And yet shalt thou be safe? such safety finds

71

The trembling lamb environèd with wolves.
Had I been there, which am a silly woman,
The soldiers should have tossed me on their pikes
Before I would have granted to that act.
But thou preferr'st thy life before thine honour:
And seeing thou dost, I here divorce myself
Both from thy table, Henry, and thy bed,
Until that act of parliament be repealed
Whereby my son is disinherited.
The northern lords that have forsworn thy colours
Will follow mine, if once they see them spread;
And spread they shall be, to thy foul disgrace
And utter ruin of the house of York.
Thus do I leave thee. Come, son, let's away;
Our army's ready: come, we'll after them.

Margaret is throwing down the gauntlet of defiance
before her husband, Henry VI. It is worth looking, as it
usually is, at the preceding passages and at the comments
of Henry after Margaret's exit. For example, preceding her
speech, Exeter says, "Here comes the queen, her looks
betray her anger. I'll steal away."

Henry says, "Exeter, so will I." And then adds, "Be
patient gentle queen."

Two grown men, and one a king, would rather leave the
room than face the woman who is bearing down on them.
Poor Henry mistakenly tells his wife that he felt
"enforced" to disinherit his son, and with the ill use of that
word brings down the full wrath of Margaret, his wife and
queen.

Here, in Margaret's "Enforced thee!" speech, is perhaps

a classic example of the man/woman in Bill's catalogue. Margaret is customarily now played by a woman, of course, but one can still imagine the power of a young male actor playing the role in the original production of the play. At times the speech is a forceful news bulletin, coming as it does toward the opening of the play. Beyond the delivery of certain news items is the over-riding strength inherent in the speech. Margaret of Anjou was by all accounts a dynamic and powerful woman, eventually going on to lead her husband's army in battle, with some success. She almost single-handedly began the Wars of the Roses between the great families and houses of York and Lancaster. Presumably, she saw the threat to her husband's position from the Yorkists, who had a very legitimate claim to the throne of England. With a demented husband and a young son to protect, Queen Margaret was not a woman to be taken lightly.

As she is represented in this speech she is a powerhouse of rhetoric and spleen. In a world often motivated by deep religious discipline and a strong alternative belief in witch-craft, she was feared by many.

Margaret might have had some idea of what was going on in the council meeting, but we have to see this as a fairly extemporized speech. Clifford has only recently left the council to tell Margaret what had transpired and that it seems her son is being disinherited. Margaret is up and into the council chamber in a few moments and firing on all cylinders on arrival.

Again, it is imperative that the actress, or the actor, keep the high rhetoric and passion under the tightest control. Margaret makes a quite cool exit from the scene and at no time does she lose control either of the moment or of what she is saying to those gathered before her. A passion, most certainly, but again not one shredded or torn to tatters.

It is too easy to get confused about this area of English history, particularly as written by this author, since he was writing mostly for the Tudors and he did not always seem to worry too much about the historic truth of what he wrote. *Richard III* is a classic example of propagandist writing to suit the powers that were dominant in Elizabethan London. Here, this Margaret is the lady who cursed poor Lord Hastings so violently that he remembers her on his way to the scaffold. She laid down several curses on Richard III in her time and in these plays of the wars between the two great northern dynasties of York and Lancaster. Margaret's husband, Henry VI, is the corpse over whom Lady Anne was caught napping by Richard, Duke of Gloucester, later Richard III, and Margaret is a small role in the play *Richard III*. The lady radiates through many plays of this era, as the actual Margaret radiated through her extraordinary life and times.

Married at fifteen or so years of age to the quite young and still sane Henry VI, Margaret of Anjou was something of a survivor and by this time in her life had been around the courts of Europe and was undoubtedly a considerable force to be reckoned with in England.

An actor approaching Margaret could garner any number of stage directions for the lady by reading through *Henry VI* (of which, I politely remind the reader, there are three installments) and seeing what others say of her. This is generally a useful exercise for any actor in any play, to learn what is said of the character one is assembling rather than what is solely said by the character, but in Margaret's case it could prove *most* useful. Just bear in mind who it is that is making the report: Gloucester and Clarence will have a different point of view than will Margaret's son, Edward, Prince of Wales. Warwick, called Kingmaker, will doubtless have several probably simultaneous and differing points of view to offer on the subject of Margaret. Warwick would have been a great spin doctor in today's political scene, keeping his career afloat by appealing to both sides of any conflict. The late-night news and cable stations of our times are filled with potential Warwicks, all jockeying for position. Is it any wonder that these plays still have currency?

WHY: To establish the rift in the court; to further extend the division between the Yorkists and the Lancastrians; to raise the ante at the beginning of the play.

WHERE: Wherever Bill imagines the scene to take place, he very specifically places the throne of England in the room. The very seat over which the argument is raging and will rage is represented there on the stage, waiting to be occupied by the fittest individual. There is much talk of "parliament" in the scene prior to Margaret's entrance, but parliaments met in several places at that time. Wherever it is, it is not to be confused with the modern chambers of parliament in Westminster. The royal families of the time had thrones in many places, and as they have today, they probably had a traveling variety.

WHO: Margaret is mostly addressing her husband, Henry VI, who was some ten years her senior. Even by this time, Henry was of very doubtful temperament and unsoundness of mind. Margaret probably has her son, the heir to

Henry's throne, tucked under her wing throughout the tirade, but the majority of her real opposition has just left the room and the scene.

OTHER: : In Act 1, scene 4, there is an interesting description of Margaret, albeit from her condemned enemy, the Duke of York. In a later scene, Queen Margaret demonstrates her power by allowing York to have his say and then cold-bloodedly assists others in stabbing him to death. She then orders York's head placed over the gates of the city for which he and his family were named. Margaret should have been running a Hollywood studio in the 1940's, perhaps she was. Some of her actions make *The Godfather* (1972) look like a story about a vicar's tea party.

I was once most fortunate to witness the late Peggy Ashcroft take us through almost the entire life of Margaret in one day. At ten o'clock on a Saturday morning, Dame Peggy began in *Henry VI, Part 1*, with the young Margaret, and on to a 2.30 p.m. matinee of *Henry VI, Part 2*. At the 7.00 p.m. performance of *Henry VI, Part 3*, we saw the great actress coming to the end of this extraordinary life as depicted in these plays. Not just for this great actress a mere matter of aging, but more a case of accumulating prowess and experience, riding the crests of triumphant waves and surviving the troughs of despair. It was an astonishing day of truly great acting from Dame Peggy and one through which she was ably supported by the amazing David Warner as Margaret's husband, the wretched lunatic Henry VI.

Glossary

YORK opposed to Lancaster.

WARWICK pronounced Worrick. Earl of Warwick, Lord Chancellor of England.

CALAIS French seaport, then in the hands of the English.

FAULCONBRIDGE a soldier and an earl of England.

THE DUKE Duke of Gloucester (Richard III to be).

ISABELLA

MEASURE FOR MEASURE   Act 2, Scene 4.
A room in the house of Lord Angelo.
Isabella

Isabella: To whom should I complain? Did I tell
  this,
Who would believe me? O perilous mouths,
That bear in them one and the self-same tongue,
Either of condemnation or approof,
Bidding the law make curtsy to their will,
Hooking both right and wrong to th' appetite,
To follow as it draws.... I'll to my brother.
Though he hath fall'n by prompture of the blood,
Yet hath he in him such a mind of honour,
That, had he twenty heads to tender down
On twenty bloody blocks, he'ld yield them up,
Before his sister should her body stoop

To such abhorr'd pollution....
Then Isabel live chaste, and brother die;
More than our brother is our chastity....
I'll tell him yet of Angelo's request,
And fit his mind to death, for his soul's rest.

I have selected some monologues which are used by Bill
to set up a scene, or to set up a play. Here, Isabella's problem is contradictory and twofold. The actor playing this
short speech from the end of the fourth scene of Act 2 of
Measure For Measure must close out the scene after having
a virtual and virtuous battle with the inappropriately
named Angelo. The problem is to register the appalling circumstances of Angelo's proposal that Isabella's brother
may live if only she will sleep with Angelo. At the same
time the actor must send the play forward with some
expectation of resolution.

To whom should Isabella complain? To whom should
the actor address this soliloquy? To the audience? That
might work, but it might also break the spell of the play.
Articulating the question to herself might at best disclose a
part of her psyche, which could provide an answer to the
poor lady's perilous dilemma.

The opening of the speech is classic. Two short, easy to
breathe but explosive questions. There then follows the
internal confusion trying to reason an answer. "O perilous
mouths" to "To follow as it draws" appears to me to be
best placed trippingly, if I may, on the tongue and with one
anguished breath.

One short (stage direction) sentence, "I'll to my brother." Then another rolling, tripping sentence through to

"pollution," which serves to drive up the emotional stakes. Two completed thoughts to lift the end of the scene and close the act.

How is the exit to be accomplished? An interesting question. By running to Brother Claudio? By moving slowly, reluctant to bring her brother the tidings? Or perhaps just by sinking to the floor in an attitude of prayer. The last might work for an audition, or even for the right production.

WHY: Angelo has left Isabella to mull over the proposition that if she sleeps with him, he will let her brother, Claudio, live. Since Isabella is sworn to a nunnery, this is for her a somewhat complex question. As Angelo has just suggested to her, she may not be readily believed if she announces to the world this dreadful proposition of his.

WHERE: A room in the house of Angelo, which Isabella must soon vacate. I have always thought it rather odd that this play is set in Vienna.

WHO: As I mentioned previously, it is the actor's choice as to who hears this speech. It is not a direct aside to the audience, I think, but it seems to be best placed in that limbo of good theatre wherein one does not quite specify exactly whom you are addressing. This is a territory common to most auditions. Indeed, it is a commonplace in too many auditions that the auditionee does not in fact know for whom he or she is auditioning. The discussion of such a sad state of affairs may be the subject of another book. Certainly, it is just as beneficial to know for whom you are giving the audition as it is useful to know in the theatre for whom you are performing. Before offering their wares young actors should feel free to find out who it is that may purchase.

OTHER: Take into consideration the morality and religion of the time. It seems almost irrational to me in the twenty-first century that a sister could think her chastity of greater value than the life of her brother (of course it might depend on the character of the brother in question). Times have changed, but for Isabella it is a massive dilemma. She clearly feels that if she remains chaste, although her brother dies as a consequence, they may both reach some heavenly state of grace, her brother, apparently, somewhat earlier than Isabella. If she submits to Angelo, both she and her brother may be sent to purgatory.

Glossary

PROMPTURE OF THE BLOOD hotheadedness.
BLOODY BLOCKS execution blocks.
ABHORR'D POLLUTION rape by Angelo.

FORD

THE MERRY WIVES OF WINDSOR Act 2, Scene 2.
A room in the Garter Inn, Windsor.
Ford

Ford: What a damned Epicurean rascal is this! My
heart is ready to crack with impatience.... Who says
this is improvident jealousy? My wife hath sent to
him, the hour is fixed, the match is made.... Would
any man have thought this? See the hell of having
a false woman: my bed shall be abused, my coffers
ransacked, my reputation gnawn at; and I shall not
only receive this villainous wrong, but stand under
the adoption of abominable terms, and by him that
does me this wrong.....Terms, names! Amaimon
sounds well; Lucifer, well; Barbason, well; yet they are
devils' additions, the names of fiends: but Cuckold!
Wittol! Cuckold! the devil himself hath not such a

name....Page is an ass, a secure ass; he will trust his
wife, he will not be jealous. I will rather trust a
Fleming with my butter, Parson Hugh the Welshman
with my cheese, an Irishman with my aqua-vitae bot-
tle, or a thief to walk my ambling gelding, than my
wife with herself.... Then she plots, then she rumi-
nates, then she devises: and what they think in their
hearts they may effect, they will break their hearts,
but they will effect....God be praised for my jealousy....Eleven o'clock the hour. I will prevent this,
detect my wife, be revenged on Falstaff, and laugh at
Page....I will about it- better three hours too soon,
than a minute too late.....Fie, fie, fie! cuckold! cuckold! cuckold!

Another closing speech, though on this occasion only a
scene closing. Ford left alone, and having concealed his
identity from Sir John Falstaff, is fairly bursting with rage
and indignation, albeit comedic rage and humorous indignation. Wonderful example of the use of staccato writing,
which underlines Ford's exasperation and for me implies
some, but not too much, sharp movement underlining the
speech: sent-hour-match...my bed-my coffers-my reputation...Amaimon-Lucifer-Barbason...plots-ruminates-devis-
es...detect-revenged-laugh...Fie, fie, fie!...cuckold! cuckold!
cuckold!

Without laboring the point, there are more than the
above quoted 1-2-3's embedded in this clever piece of comedy writing. Again, I think simplifying the rhythm allows
the actor to fully concentrate on getting the speech across
to the audience.

Taking in the audience with this speech will develop valuable comedic bonds of sympathy with the men in the theatre, or at the audition.

WHY:To enhance our understanding of Ford's position by showing ourselves as other see us.

WHERE: A room at the Garter Inn in Windsor, a small town thirty miles west of London which has for many centuries been a second home to many of England's royal families.

WHO: To himself? To his audience? Or to the disguise he has just been using to deceive Falstaff?

OTHER: Ford has been under some duress in the previous scene since he has been required to sustain the character of Master Brook, and it might be most likely after such a strain that when he does finally burst out as Ford his outburst is the greater.

Glossary

EPICUREAN After Epicurus, the Greek philosopher who gave allowance to the thought that pleasure was the highest form of goodness, but who himself apparently enjoyed nothing more than good water and fresh bread. Not far off the mark as a description of Falstaff, apart from the reference to appreciating bread and water.

AMAIMON a mighty devil.

BARBASON a prince of devils.

WITTOL wit old, cuckold.

FLEMING Lowlander of Europe. The English are invariably rude about foreigners.

PARSON HUGH....CHEESE Interesting stage direction for the actor playing Hugh. A dig at the Welsh, who were still bothersome to the English at the time of the writing.

AQUA-VITAE Literally, water of life, but in fact used to describe hard liquor, perhaps brandy. A hip flask? Does Ford drink? As with the remarks about cheese, this allows another sure-fire laugh, this time on the subject of the Irish and alcohol.

I WILL ABOUT IT I will get on with it.

TITANIA

A MIDSUMMER NIGHTS DREAM Act 2, Scene 1.
A palace wood, Athens.

Titania

Titania: These are the forgeries of jealousy:
And never, since the middle summer's spring,
Met we on hill, in dale, forest, or mead,
By pavèd fountain, or by rushy brook,
Or in the beachèd margent of the sea,
To dance our ringlets to the whistling wind,
But with thy brawls thou hast disturbed our sport.
Therefore, the winds, piping to us in vain,
As in revenge, have sucked up from the sea
Contagious fogs: which falling in the land,
Hath every pelting river made so proud
That they have overborne their continents:
The ox hath therefore stretched his yoke in vain,
The ploughman lost his sweat, and the green corn

Hath rotted ere his youth attained a beard;
The fold stands empty in the drownèd field,
And crows are fatted with the murrion flock,
The nine men's morris is filled up with mud,
And the quaint mazes in the wanton green
For lack of tread are undistinguishable.
The human mortals want their winter cheer;
No night is now with hymn or carol blest;
Therefore the moon, the governess of floods,
Pale in her anger, washes all the air,
That rheumatic diseases do abound.
And thorough this distemperature we see
The seasons alter: hoary-headed frosts
Fall in the fresh lap of the crimson rose,
And on old Hiems' thin and icy crown
An odorous chaplet of sweet summer buds
Is, as in mockery, set. The spring, the summer,
The childing autumn, angry winter, change
Their wonted liveries; and the mazèd world,
By their increase, now knows not which is which.
And this same progeny of evil comes
From our debate, from our dissension:
We are their parents and original.

Titania and Oberon, long known to each other, have just now met for the first time in the play. The first thing we hear about Titania is that she is described by Oberon as "proud." We might take that with a pinch of salt. She begins immediately to leave Oberon's presence, but he keeps her in the scene with more insults, calling her rash and wanton and asking if he is not her lord.

Titania does not agree, but neither does she deny that

Oberon is her lord. She goes on to throw a spleenful attack at Oberon on the grounds of his relationship with the mortal, Hippolyta. In reply to this, of course, Oberon attempts to rebuff her attack with the suggestion that Titania is in love with Theseus, duke of Athens, who is the mortal betrothed to Hippolyta. Hence to "These are the forgeries of jealousy...."

Titania launches into a veritable weather report concerning the catastrophes that transpire every time she and Oberon meet. She paints a pastoral picture of how, when she and her friends are enjoying themselves, Oberon has to come brawling and disturb their sport. To hear Titania, Oberon's power is so prodigious that we might compare it to that of El Nino, that it can change the weather pattern of their world, cause flood and famine and totally disrupt everything.

Is Titania really so angry here at Oberon? If she is, how amazing that she may summon such brilliant language in her rage. Is this the writer once more showing us how to temper our passion? It certainly would temper anyone's passion to have to enforce it with such a colorful and rich collection of words and images.

At the last moment having appeared to condemn Oberon, Titania includes herself in the making of the disaster she has depicted:

"And this same progeny of evils comes
From *our* debate, from *our* dissension;
We are their *parents* and original."

I don't suggest you stress the words shown here in italics. I am only pointing out that here is not, in the final analysis, a criticism solely of Oberon.

WHY: The meeting of Oberon and Titania is one of the most memorable in all of Bill's writing. Stiff with irony and caustic commentary on their relationship, these two must be the most practical of fairies. Their relationship is, I think, far more real than any mortal relationship in the play. It is as real as Strindberg, and like many characters in Strindberg and his plagiarists, these two are fighting over another being, a changeling child, who may be as much a part of their combined imaginations as that of George and Martha's in *Who's Afraid of Virginia Woolf?*

Unlike that of many other couples in Bill's plays, the argument of Titania and Oberon is conducted on a very high plane of English language. Here Titania shows much presence of mind to be able to make this kind of verbal attack on a loved one.

WHERE: A grove of trees near Athens, the capital of Greece. Night.

WHO: No problem. A direct attack aimed at Oberon and finally at herself.

OTHER: Of course, Titania knows that Oberon is after the changeling child and that her "lord" hopes to make her so angry that he will somehow be able to abduct the boy. This thought alone will help to give the anger the temperance suggested by Hamlet. The temperance that any such speech should have.

Glossary

MEAD meadow.

MARGENT border, margin.

NINE MEN'S MORRIS children's game plot. (Think of the layout for hopscotch, which is similar.)

HIEM'S winter's. From the Latin, *hiemalis*, pertainingn to winter.

CHAPLET garland.

MURRION FLOCK sometimes murrain, a disease of cattle and sheep.

THOROUGH through.

CHILDING breeding, fruitful, pregnant.

LET DISCRETION
BE YOUR TUTOR

In the first two sections I have selected some pieces
that require powerful delivery and much passion.
In this third section are some speeches with which
the actor can engage a more reasonable and less
oratorical approach.

JAQUES

AS YOU LIKE IT Act 2, Scene 7.
The Forest of Arden.
Jaques

Jaques: All the world's a stage,
And all the men and women merely players;
They have their exits and their entrances,
And one man in his time plays many parts,
His acts being seven ages.... At first the infant,
Mewling and puking in the nurse's arms:
Then the whining school-boy, with his satchel
And shining morning face, creeping like snail
Unwillingly to school: and then the lover,
Sighing like furnace, with a woeful ballad
Made to his mistress' eyebrow: then a soldier,
Full of strange oaths and bearded like the pard,
Jealous in honour, sudden and quick in quarrel.
Seeking the bubble reputation

Even in the cannon's mouth: and then the justice,
In fair round belly with good capon lined,
With eyes severe and beard of formal cut,
Full of wise saws and modern instances,
And so he plays his part.... The sixth age shifts
Into the lean and slippered pantaloon,
With spectacles on nose and pouch on side,
His youthful hose, well saved, a world too wide
For his shrunk shank, and his big manly voice,
Turning again toward childish treble, pipes
And whistles in his sound.... Last scene of all,
That ends this strange eventful history,
Is second childishness, and mere oblivion
Sans teeth, sans eyes, sans taste, sans everything.

As with the Chorus from *Henry V*, this speech is so well
known that it might present a veritable minefield for the
actor. Fortunately, it is so brilliantly and economically
written that however many times we hear the "Ages of
Man," it never ceases to entertain, inform, and amuse.

Jaques could have made a fortune popping on at the end
of *Sixty Minutes* and putting the world to rights. In fact, it
might be interesting to cast around the networks and see
which of the pundits suits you best as a role model, if you
choose to work on this speech. Perhaps William Buckley?
Mr. B. has been wandering around in his own little forest
for some years now, accumulating thoughts and imparting
them to all and sundry. David Frost? Mort Sahl? Dennis
Miller?

Jaques must be a man of some experience to come up
with such a freewheeling and accurate description of life.

Maybe it is the magical number seven which continues to give this speech such power over the years.

Interesting questions. In which of Jaques' "ages" does he himself belong? How may the actor choose to play him? One would think he must be beyond the soldier, and maybe beyond the lawyer. Is he in the sixth stage of "slippered pantaloon"? Surely not as old as the "Last scene of all," since there seems to be nothing particularly of "second childishness" about any of Jaques in this play.

Certainly, Jaques is still young enough to survive in the Forest of Arden with the duke's outlawed group, so one would imagine he is quite fit of body. He is very fit of mind too. Anyone trying to hold his place with this group would need his full assembly of wits about him. Jaques seems very much to be the spiritual leader of the exiled men in the forest, rather in the mold of Friar Tuck in relation to Robin Hood's merry men. Though clearly Jaques is not attached to any religious order other than that of his own invention. He might have had some experience with a religious order at some time in his life, and one imagines from his understanding of the soldier that he has fought in one or two campaigns.

It rather depends on how you want to depict him, but as I suggested, there are ample role models for this character around today. Granted not too many with his sense of poetry or his wry wit, but Jaques is alive and well and living on many a campus, airing his views in many a media circus.

WHY: There seems to be a technical reason here for the speech, in that Orlando is sent off to bring Adam on, and that means some time must be allowed to elapse. What an amazing vamp-till-ready this speech then becomes. Of course, the speech provides Jaques with a chance to establish himself further with the exiled group in the forest and with the audience in the theatre. He has a chance to show how brilliantly and how quickly he thinks. The banished duke has only just introduced the theme of theatre into the conversation, and Jaques is able to pick up on it and paint a great word picture of life as merely a series of roles played. In fact, Jaques even snaps into the duke's previous line, and he is so ready to engage in the argument that he picks up the speech on a half line.

WHERE: The Forest of Arden. Winter, if we are to believe the ensuing song of Amiens, "Blow, blow thou winter wind."

WHO: Another natural audience to hear this speech, as Jaques is clearly playing it to the other members of the duke's exiled party. Jaques, of course, is something of a court jester for this group but more sophisticated than most court jesters, and it is probably with this in mind that Bill sets up later in the play such a good verbal battle between the one-time professional jester Touchstone and Jaques. Indeed, you might want to look at Jaques' previous speech in this same scene, where he discusses Touchstone, or, as he calls him, the "fool" he met in the forest.

OTHER: Consonants! I mean by that exclamation to suggest that the actor's tongue might appear to be working overtime with the facility that Jaques has acquired from long experience. I think the author is asking the actor to be very specific vocally with this philosophical essay. Jaques seems to me to be a somewhat languid creature, but he has been talking in this manner for many years and knows exactly where to take his improvisation. It is true, I am sure, that Jaques might feel at times a little above his current audience of exiled courtiers, but nevertheless, he does not talk down to them; some of these courtiers he has known for many years, and there is mutual respect in this group. Jaques knows he will be listened to. He loves to be listened to, and so he should; he speaks very well indeed. He is a master of cadence.

Glossary

MEWLING crying like a cat.

PARD leopard, panther.

SAWS axioms, adages, sayings.

SANS French: without, missing.

SHRUNK SHANK thin leg.

PANTALOON Commedia dell' arte character and ancient saint revered in Venice. Any elderly man who might be ridiculed by some, usually younger, people.

ROSALIND

AS YOU LIKE IT Epilogue.
Rosalind

Rosalind: It is not the fashion to see the lady the epilogue: but it is no more un-handsome than to see the lord the prologue. If it be true that good wine needs no bush, 'tis true that a good play needs no epilogue: yet to good wine they do use good bushes; and good plays prove the better by the help of good epilogues.... What a case am I in then, that am neither a good epilogue nor cannot insinuate with you in the behalf of a good play! I am not furnished like a beggar; therefore to beg will not become me: my way is to conjure you, and I'll begin with the women. I charge you, O women, for the love you bear to men, to like as much of this play as please you: and I charge you, O men, for the love you bear to women- as I perceive by your simp'ring none of you hates them- that between you and the women the play may please. If I were a woman, I would kiss as many of you as had beards that pleased me, complexions that liked me, and breaths that I defied not: and, I am sure, as many as have good beards, or good faces, or sweet breaths, will for my kind offer, when I make curtsy, bid me farewell.

Here is an interesting speech for the younger men reading this book and I daresay one or two ladies might be tempted to play it as an audition speech, though in truth it has serious ramifications that mitigate against its being played by a lady. At least, there is a flat suggestion in the speech that the speaker is not a woman:

"If I were a woman..."

The speech comprises a remarkable and lighthearted assessment of the evening's entertainment, with the polite and sometimes necessary hint of apology many epilogues and some prologues carry.

Of course the speech presents a direct frontal attack on the audience in the theatre, as is the case with most epilogues. For me these moments in theatre are often themselves the most rewarding when we see the actors divesting themselves of the parts they have been playing all evening. No less interesting for an audition, in that such a speech as this allows the viewer to see something of the actor as well as something of the acting. This epilogue could be a useful vehicle with which to persuade a producer or casting director that you are worthy of his or her interest. The speech, at least, is a worthwhile exercise for the actor in expressing ease, affability, and charm .

Jean Anouilh, the superb French playwright, suggests, moreover, that one of the most difficult things for an actor to accomplish is making an entrance and having made it successfully, the most difficult thing is then to make a successful exit. The last three strides which will take the actor off the stage are sometimes very hard to gauge. There is an art in placing such an epilogue.

WHY: It is good manners to be at the door when one's guests are departing, and in that ritualistic sense the speech is there to provide a bridge back to reality.

In playing the speech in a performance the actor might use some artifice in moving swiftly in at the end of the play to frustrate the audience's applause, the applause therefore being the greater when it is released after the word "farewell." Such a plan may also give a certain charge to the beginning of the speech.

WHERE: No-man's-land (and, strictly speaking, perhaps no-woman's-land), that limbo of space and time provided at the end of many successful theatrical performances. There is no longer the tradition in most theatres of a leading member of the cast making a curtain speech, which personally I regret, as I always thought it was an interesting bridge both for the acting company and the audience who had witnessed the play.

WHO: The audience. In audition the casting director, the producer, or the director.

OTHER: Presentational acting. "If I were a woman": the actor here is clearly not in character. Rosalind may not say "If I were a woman" even as Ganymede, and by this time the actor is dressed, as at the beginning of the play, as a woman. It must be a thrust played from the point of view of the actor himself, not the character he was playing during the evening, hence the leading comment concerning its not being fashionable to see the "lady the epilogue." If I were a female I would still play the speech for some auditions. If I were to direct *As You Like It*, I think I would not cast ladies in the play.

The all-male production produced by the National Theatre of Great Britain at the Old Vic in 1967 left me with great difficulty in subsequently watching ladies play this text. The utterly remarkable Rosalind of the mercurial Ronald Pickup will never be erased from my memory, nor I suspect from the memories of those thousands who observed his astonishing performance in that production. As an historical footnote, this might be the place to mention that Mr. Pickup was ably supported on the distaff side by Charles Kay as a somewhat sullen, saucy, and bespectacled Celia; the late Richard Kay as a far too beautiful Phoebe, and that prince of Wales Anthony Hopkins as a flaxen-pigtailed Audrey. (You see, anything is possible with this author.) All four actors, each in his way, were brilliant. The remainder of the company, excellent.

Glossary

EPILOGUE It was more the custom for a male character to speak an epilogue.

GOOD WINE NEEDS NO BUSH Good products do not need advertisement. The ivy bush, either painted on an inn sign or an actual bush, was often a symbol for the selling of wine.

SONNET 113

Since I left you, mine eye is in my mind,
And that which governs me to go about,
Doth part his function and is partly blind,
Seems seeing, but effectually is out:
For it no form delivers to the heart
Of bird, of flower, or shape which it doth latch,
Of his quick objects hath the mind no part,
Nor his own vision holds what it doth catch:
For if it see the rud'st or gentlest sight,
The most sweet favour or deformed'st creature,
The mountain, or the sea, the day, or night,
The crow, or dove, it shapes them to your feature:
Incapable of more, replete with you,
My most true mind thus maketh mine untrue.

Sometimes it helps you, and the people for whom you
are auditioning, if you throw in a short piece of work. For

this purpose, among others, I suggest a look through the sonnets.

Obviously, with such a canvas before the actor, something more personal and suitable is likely to be found, but this sonnet, 113, has a quiet but emotional intensity to it and expresses such a longing that it is very actable. Like some other speeches in this book, this sonnet, is, I think, a great exercise for the working actor. It will surely keep the diction in good order, and be a constant reminder that subtlety in acting is becoming a lost part of the craft.

WHY: Therapy for a onetime love, a deceased partner, a former friend.

WHERE: Your choice, as it always is in this book, but here with no restrictions outside the content of the fourteen lines.

WHY: Your inner self.

OTHER: Keep it simple. "Speak the speech."

Glossary

LATCH moisten.

DUKE OF BURGUNDY

HENRY V Act 5, Scene 2.
France: A royal palace.
Duke of Burgundy, Henry, Katharine

Burgundy: My duty to you both, on equal love....
Great Kings of France and England: that I have laboured
With all my wits, my pains, and strong endeavours,
To bring your most imperial majesties
Unto this bar and royal interview,
Your mightiness on both parts best can witness....
Since then my office hath so far prevailed,
That face to face, and royal eye to eye,
You have congreeted: let it not disgrace me,
If I demand before this royal view,
What rub, or what impediment there is,
Why that the naked, poor, and mangled Peace,
Dear nurse of arts, plenties, and joyful births,

Should not in this best garden of the world,
Our fertile France, put up her lovely visage?
Alas, she hath from France too long been chased,
And all her husbandry doth lie on heaps,
Corrupting in it's own fertility.
Her vine, the merry cheerer of the heart,
Unprunèd dies: her hedges even-pleached,
Like prisoners wildly over-grown with hair,
Put forth disordered twigs: her fallow leas
The darnel, hemlock, and rank fumitory
Doth root upon, while that the coulter rusts
That should deracinate such savagery:
The even mead, that erst brought sweetly forth
The freckled cowslip, burnet, and green clover,
Wanting the scythe, all uncorrected, rank,
Conceives by idleness, and nothing teems
But hateful docks, rough thistles, kecksies, burs,
Losing both beauty and utility;
And as our vineyards, fallows, meads, and hedges,
Defective in their natures, grow to wildness,
Even so our houses, and ourselves, and children,
Have lost, or do not learn, for want of time,
The sciences that should become our country;
But grow like savages, as soldiers will
That nothing do but meditate on blood,
To swearing and stern looks, diffused attire,
And everything that seems unnatural.
Which to reduce into our former favour
You are assembled: and my speech entreats,
That I may know the let, why gentle Peace
Should not expel these inconveniences,
And bless us with her former qualities.

A great peacemaking speech this, from the pen of our author and through the mouth of Burgundy. The speech should be in the United Nations charter since it still perfectly exemplifies the ridiculous waste caused by any war. Afghanistan, Cambodia, Congo, Ethiopia, Rwanda, Somalia, Tibet, Vietnam, to say nothing of Bosnia, and too many other places to mention that have been similarly relandscaped by wild men and women on the loose with weaponry.

Something of what is sometimes called a "list" here, but it is a rather brilliantly contrived list of the topographical and social effects of war fully waged. It is always useful practice to work on a "list" and to find ways to stop its being just that and no more. The thinking actor will allow us to believe that Burgundy is saying this for the first time; although, of course, in this instance he could well have previously written down his main points, because it is something of a political speech.

Burgundy's problem here, or one of his problems, is that he has brought these two warhorses, England and France, to the trough, from which he hopes they will lap up a peaceful outcome. Can he make them drink?

Burgundy's dukedom has clearly suffered because of the recent war, and the time he spends on the description of the countryside around is well spent if he can drive home his point of view to these thickheads, one of whom, incidentally (the king of France), was certifiable.

It is the speech of a land lover, or even maybe a farmer, and one must remember that almost everything Burgundy mentions here would have been seen, picked, dried, eaten, or stored by almost every member of an Elizabethan audience. The world is a stage, we are told elsewhere in *As You*

Like It; here the world is a garden, and both Bill and Burgundy knew that they were talking to an audience of gardeners.

Burgundy's point would be well taken. The people of the land of which Burgundy speaks have lost their livelihood and their way of life to the wild tangles that once were arable fields that supported them and their families. It is almost as though the people are secondary, and even a modern audience will be able to identify with the theme of the speech; certainly a sixteenth century audience would have. It has always been known that it takes much time for land to be reclaimed, and, as we still see, land sometimes can never be restored to its former productive state.

This author was in such great harmony with the natural world around him that were he alive today, he would surely be protesting the loss of the Brazilian rain forest, other despoliation of the Amazon Basin, and global warming. Perhaps Burgundy is a medieval Ralph Nader.

WHY: Burgundy's mission is as peacemaker. He seems to me to be a strong man who, after the obvious niceties of introducing the warring parties, wants to get on with the job at hand. This could be an informal, sleeves-up, Camp David meeting or a full and more official assembly, but what is clear in any circumstance is the undoubted authority of the Duke of Burgundy. Though not a king, he appears to be quite the equal of both Henry of England and Charles of France.

WHERE: A large room in a French palace. One imagines that Burgundy has come to the ground being fought over, but I suppose that the meeting could take place on the more politically neutral soil of Burgundy itself. I would settle for France.

WHO: A court full of French and English noblemen and their ladies, some of whom are later delegated to do the actual work of implementing the peace treaty, while Henry stays to propose to Katharine, princess of France.

OTHER: Whether it is historically true or not, don't lose sight of the fact that Bill has invested Burgundy with great knowledge of the subject about which he speaks. I suggested earlier, it is almost the speech of a well-informed minister of agriculture, or at least an experienced land owner or estate manager.

Glossary

PLEACHED intertwined.
FUMITORY delicate herb.
COULTER blade of a plough.
DERACINATE uproot.
DARNEL genus of grass.
HEMLOCK poisonous parsely, sometimes used in a mild form as a sedative and for other medicinal purposes.
MEAD meadows or fields.
COWSLIP form of primrose.
BURNET wild rose, from which we have extracted the word "brunette."
KECKSIES more hemlocks.
BURS prickly outer skin of some seed pods.

PORTIA

THE MERCHANT OF VENICE Act 4, Scene 1.
A court of justice.

*Portia, Shylock, Duke of Venice, Antonio, Bassanio,
and others*

Portia: The quality of mercy is not strained,
It droppeth as the gentle rain from heaven
Upon the place beneath. It is twice blessed:
It blesseth him that gives, and him that takes,
'Tis mightiest in the mightiest, it becomes
The thronèd monarch better than his crown:
His sceptre shows the force of temporal power,
The attribute to awe and majesty,
Wherein doth sit the dread and fear of kings:
But mercy is above this sceptred sway,
It is enthronèd in the hearts of kings,
It is an attribute to God himself,

And earthly power doth then show likest God's
When mercy seasons justice. Therefore, Jew,
Though justice be thy plea, consider this,
That in the course of justice none of us
Should see salvation: we do pray for mercy,
And that same prayer doth teach us all to render
The deeds of mercy. I have spoke thus much,
To mitigate the justice of thy plea,
Which if thou follow, this strict court of Venice
Must needs give sentence 'gainst the merchant there.

In the male garments of a doctor of civil law, which have
been borrowed from her old friend Bellario, Portia has just
arrived in Venice to plead for the release of Antonio, the
Venetian Merchant in question, whom Portia has never
met. At first unable to tell the difference between Antonio
and Shylock, she asks a few rudimentary questions and
then launches into what has become one of the most
famous speeches in the canon.

I think that this is possibly an overused speech at auditions but I have included it here because I have only ever
seen it given the most benign reading. Further, in my opinion, too often in performance the actor is inclined to
become soft right here at the outset of the trial. In my opinion, fatal!

I once witnessed this scene being played by a fifteen-
year- old schoolboy in a school program and of course it
worked like a charm for him because he was able to play it
for real.

Any respectable actress may also take a more realistic
line on the speech. How could Portia be so good an attor-

ney? Is she studying the law between suitors at Belmont? Possibly, but not probably. Where has she attained her courtroom manner? Or is she just hoping against hope that what she says comes out right? She must surely be making this speech up as she goes along, which provides the auditionee with a chance to appear to be extemporizing.

This is such a much more interesting speech if we can believe that it is "happening" in the moments, not being recited, in the manner in which it too often appears to be, which in Bill's words might be "too tame." *

The actor playing Portia may wish to contemplate just how vindictive the lady is once she has turned the balance in her favor. What talk of the "quality of mercy" is there from Portia once she releases the idea of Shylock's not being empowered by his bond to take anything but one pound of flesh and not one single drop of blood? The last is a rhetorical question on my part since there is no mercy shown at all. None whatsoever. This Portia is a very intractable lady. Ask the prince of Morocco, or any of those other Belmont suitors. Portia, relentlessly and without mercy, eventually steps all over Shylock's estate, as previously in this play her now new husband, Bassanio, and his friends have stepped all over Shylock's family, staff, and home.

One's "discretion" may lead one to suppose that Portia has been schooled by Bellario before arriving in Venice, to set a trap with the chat about mercy: in which case one cannot play it for sincerity without making Portia a stunning actress. If, on the other hand, Portia gets the idea her-

---

* "Be not too tame neither, but let your own discretion be your tutor." Don't forget those earlier acting notes through the voice of Hamlet.

self of not taking any more than one pound of flesh, one could at least argue on her behalf that the newlywed became just a little carried away in the moment. Either way, the quality of mercy speech is a minefield, and cannot be centered on, or truly emanate from, a simply sentimental heart, in which manner it is invariably played.

WHY: If Portia has premeditated, she is baiting a trap; if not, she is making up an interesting speech about mercy, which, when push comes to shove, she has no intention of allowing herself to follow. Whatever, I feel that the lady may well be driven by desire to please Bassanio; but she is not sincere in this trial scene. Portia is not very sincere anywhere in the play, I think. Poor Shylock could hardly have come across a more cruel and vindictive group of Christians if he had stumbled into a group of knights on crusade or inadvertently arrived in Madrid in the middle of the Spanish Inquisition.

WHERE: Accepting the fact that any venue at which the duke of Venice wishes to convene his court may be a suitable place for a trial, this scene could take place almost anywhere. The noted theatre director Jonathan Miller once set this scene in a dimly-lit boardroom, to which it seemed the duke had been called from a weekend in the country and who had hastily convened a few clerks with whom to try the case in camera. The idea worked handsomely, and for once, with the relative gloom of the atmosphere Dr. Miller established, the audience was more readily able to believe what the people in the court must believe, that Portia and Nerissa are young males.

WHO: Wherever the duke decides to have his court, there should be several witnesses in addition to Antonio, his friends, and Shylock, to whom the speech is clearly directed. There is here in this scene, as with the play generally, a triple audience to whom Portia may play. The duke is clearly one important element; the clerks and others around the trial are another; and then there are those despicable cohorts of Antonio, Bassanio, and Gratiano. The latter, being of a rather coarse nature, need very little prompting from the lady of Belmont.

OTHER: I have always thought that Portia and her so-called Christian friends were particularly beastly around this area of the play, and frankly they are not too pleasant for me elsewhere. At no time in the play in my recollection does this lady show any form of "mercy." There is no mercy earlier in the play for Morocco, no mercy for Arragon, nor for any of the vast number of much ridiculed suitors who are at one time stacked up outside Portia's front door at Belmont. Portia deserves everything she gets in falling for the money-grabbing Bassanio. I suspect that their marriage, like most of the marriages in Bill's writing, will be short-lived or unhappy, probably both. As apparently was the author's.

Glossary

MITIGATE ease.
THE MERCHANT THERE Antonio.

HELENA

A MIDSUMMER NIGHT'S DREAM Act 1, Scene 1.
The palace of Theseus, duke of Athens.
Helena

Helena: How happy some o'er other some can be!
Through Athens I am thought as fair as she,
But what of that? Demetrius thinks not so:
He will not know what all but he do know.
And as he errs, doting on Hermia's eyes,
So I, admiring of his qualities.
Things base and vile, holding no quantity,
Love can transpose to form and dignity.
Love looks not with the eyes, but with the mind:
And therefore is winged Cupid painted blind.
Nor hath Love's mind of any judgment taste:
Wings and no eyes figure unheedy haste.
And therefore is Love said to be a child:

Because in choice he is so oft beguiled.
As waggish boys in game themselves forswear,
So the boy Love is perjured every where;
Fore ere Demetrius looked on Hermia's eyne,
He hailed down oaths that he was only mine.
And when this hail some heat from Hermia felt,
So he dissolved, and showers of oaths did melt.
I will go tell him of fair Hermia's flight:
Then to the wood will he to-morrow night
Pursue her: and for this intelligence
If I have thanks, it is a dear expense:
But herein mean I to enrich my pain,
To have his sight thither and back again.

Considering her youth, and her extreme anguish at finding herself abused and ignored by Demetrius, this speech of
Helena's early in the play is a very well brought-about
argument. By rationalizing her position and thereby giving
herself some hope of recapturing her boy friend, Helena is
able here to motivate herself quite well, and at the same
time set up some comedic expectations for the audience.

Here again we are shown someone of intellectual ability
who before long will be groveling and thrashing about in a
complete delirium of uncontrolled emotions.

There is a hint of jealousy at the beginning, with
"thought as fair as she" and "doting on Hermia's eyes,"
but Helena overcomes the feeling and outlines her situation very well.

I think it is delightfully immature of Helena to imagine
that by telling Demetrius that Hermia is about to elope she
will in some way regain his affection. Of course it is a wish

fulfilled, but Helena can hardly claim responsibility here for the outcome of a situation that will be so dominated by the subterranean thoughts and superhuman deeds both of mortals and of fairies.

WHY: To establish the plot. To demonstrate the quite friendly rivalry between Hermia and Helena, and the familiarity of both ladies with Demetrius. To show us the more rational side of Helena, since we are going to see her bent colossally out of shape before she is returned at the end the evening to some state of grace and to her lover. Additionally, the scene will remind the audience in the theatre that they were young once, or that they are perhaps in a situation similar to Helena's, if they are young enough.

WHERE: The rooms or grounds of the same palace where the induction of the play took place; somewhere within the city walls of Athens, Greece.

WHO: If I were to play Helena, though in truth I am not sufficiently tall to do so, I would be inclined to play the speech to the house and hope to establish a sympathy for the character and a strong bond with the audience, which would help me later in the play.

OTHER: It is never an accident that Bill writes a character up into this very well reasoned thinking. Imagine how much funnier it is that a sophisticated, intelligent, seemingly clear-thinking young woman of the court should fall into such desperate straits as Helena will eventually fall into than it would be if Helena were some low-life bawd. Again we have Bill on a major theme: There but for the grace of God go I; and maybe half the courtiers of Elizabeth's entourage who might be gathered to watch the play. Everyone has problems, we are reminded, not just us poor sods sitting here in the cheap seats of the theatre. Very good therapy for the audience, to understand that; to say nothing of the therapeutic value for the courtiers and the actor playing Helena.

Glossary

DEMETRIUS young male friend of Helena.
HERMIA young female friend of the lanky Helena. Hermia is shorter than Helena.
EYNE eyes.

THE PRINCESS OF FRANCE

LOVE'S LABOUR'S LOST Act 2, Scene 1.
Navarre: The King's Park
*The Princess of France, Rosaline, Maria,
Katherine, Boyet, Lords, and other attendants*

The Princess of France: Good Lord Boyet, my
        beauty, though but mean,
Needs not the painted flourish of your praise:
Beauty is bought by judgment of the eye,
Not utt'red by base sale of chapmen's tongues.
I am less proud to hear you tell my worth
Than you much willing to be counted wise
In spending your wit in the praise of mine.
But now to task the tasker - good Boyet,
You are not ignorant, all-telling fame
Doth noise abroad Navarre hath made a vow,
Till painful study shall outwear three years,
No woman may approach his silent court:

Therefore to's seemeth it a needful course,
Before we enter his forbidden gates,
To know his pleasure; and in that behalf,
Bold of your worthiness, we single you
As our best-moving fair solicitor.
Tell him, the daughter of the King of France,
On serious business, craving quick dispatch,
Importunes personal conference with his Grace.
Haste, signify so much, while we attend,
Like humble-visaged suitors, his high will.

Here is a gracious speech, requiring some "discretion."
The Princess, bothered as usual by her equerry, the florid
Boyet, admonishes him for over-praising her and then asks
him to do a little research concerning exactly what
Navarre is up to with his court. Is it true that there has
been a vow of abstinence decided upon by Ferdinand and
the others?

That in essence is what the speech is about. Of course,
being written by this playwright, it has a beautiful and var-
ied road paved with fine words to assist us along the way
to establishing its objective.

Another aspect of the part is that Bill was writing for an
audience and a time in which conversation and the use of
words was of paramount importance. Elizabethan writers
were not plagued by the demands of the twenty-second
sound bite, or by when they had to place the commercial.
Hence the company and the playwright could afford the
time to luxuriate, as is the case here, with what might otherwise seem a very mundane speech. An actor may only
delight in the playing of such things as

my beauty, though but mean,
Needs not the painted flourish of your praise.

To say nothing of the following barb about "chapmen's tongues."

Today, of necessity, an actor would be given only the straight statement, probably simply asking Boyet to "knock it off," or at best asking him not to be so colorful in his compliments. Here Bill slips the word "beauty" into the sentence, which gives him a bridge and a thought that will carry the Princess of France into her speech.

Thus we learn so much more about one of our leading characters: that she is courtly, wise, witty, beautiful but not vain, and that she has some control over her subordinates. We may also learn something of the lady's attitude toward Ferdinand and men in general.

WHY: To introduce the Princess of France into the play. It is her first speech.

To help the plot along. To establish her position in the play and her authority on the play and in her court. To set up Boyet.

WHERE: Again, this scene appears to be set in an open space adjacent to the court of the king of Navarre. The ladies and their train have apparently just arrived.

WHO: The Princess is clearly talking to Boyet, but she is just as clearly speaking in front of her retinue and her three main ladies-in-waiting. Boyet is a mark for these four ladies, and while they are most comfortable with his functions for them, they nevertheless get a great deal of fun out of chastising Boyet for his mannered and florid use of body and words. The Princess is generous enough to redress the balance of her opening comments when she suggests late in the speech that Boyet is their "best-moving, fair solicitor."

OTHER: Don't miss the humor in little things, like "forbidden gates," "his pleasure," "craving quick dispatch," "Importunes." The Princess of France in this play is rarely talking about what she seems to be talking about. Her comments often appear to be riddled with sexual innuendo, which actually I think they are.

See the manner in which this good lady talks with her forester a little later in the play, Act 4, Scene 1. Maybe you will think there that the Princess did not just become a sparkling, somewhat ribald wit solely for the "shooting scene." Her wit is a part of her basic character, and it is evident here at the outset of the play.

Glossary

BOYET   equerry to the Princess.

CHAPMEN   servants.

TO'S   to us.

SOLICITOR   Is Boyet actually "soliciting"? I think he is, but it is probably a playful double entendre for the Princess. Nothing to be done in an audition context, but I would be most put out if in performance as Boyet, I did not take a huge laugh off this word "solicitor" here.

CLIFFORD

HENRY VI, PART 3 Act 2, Scene 6.
A field of battle near Towton, in Yorkshire.
A loud alarum. Enter Clifford, wounded

Clifford: Here burns my candle out; ay, here it dies,
Which, whiles it lasted, gave King Henry light.
O Lancaster, I fear thy overthrow
More than my body's parting with my soul!
My love and fear glued many friends to thee;
Impairing Henry, strength'ning misproud York;
The common people swarm like flies;
And whither fly the gnats but to the sun?
And who shines now but Henry's enemies?
O Phoebus, hadst thou never given consent
That Phaethon should check thy fiery steeds,
Thy burning car never had scorched the earth!
And, Henry, hadst thou swayed as kings should do,

Or as thy father and his father did,
Giving no ground unto the house of York,
They never then had sprung like summer flies;
I and ten thousand in this luckless realm
Had left no mourning widows for our death;
And thou this day hadst kept thy chair in peace.
For what doth cherish weeds but gentle air?
And what makes robbers bold but too much lenity?
Bootless are plaints, and cureless are my wounds;
No way to fly, nor strength to hold out flight:
The foe is merciless, and will not pity:
For at their hands I have deserved no pity.
The air hath got into my deadly wounds,
And much effuse of blood doth make me faint.
Come, York and Richard, Warwick and the rest;
I stabbed your fathers' bosoms, split my breast.

Here, I think, is an interesting problem. Like the Bloody
Captain in *Macbeth*, Clifford must maintain his energy
and momentum, though only long enough to faint dead
away at the end of the speech. What a delightful dilemma.
How much energy may the actor expend on the speech?
When does the final faint begin to kick in? How breath-
less? Clifford tells us right at the front of the speech that he
has more or less had it. In fact, he dies within seconds of
finishing the last line, prophetically expiring at precisely
the moment when Warwick suggests that by now Clifford
must be "surely dead."

Not quite the world flashing before Clifford in these, his
final moments of this life, but perhaps it is that last burst
of energy one sometimes hears of reported by a soldier

dying on a battlefield or by an athlete running a great race. Valery Borzov, the great sprinter from the USSR, gave one of the very best acting lessons one evening in 1969 at the White City Stadium in London. Borzov, a world-record holder, was then billed as the fastest man on the planet. He easily won the hundred meter race in which he was competing on that crystal clear night. In a post-race interview Borzov was complimented by a British interviewer who suggested that he had run a brilliant race. Indeed, the interviewer went on to suggest that it was a "perfect" exhibition of modern sprinting technique. I was no longer an athlete but I shall always recall the sprinter's reply. He countered with the thought that he was not satisfied with his performance: " I was not perfect, as I did not do everything I could have within the allotted distance." "But," the interviewer said, " You won the race so easily and you broke the European record." "Maybe," said Mr. Borzov, "but did you not notice that I was still running some twenty or thirty yards beyond the finish line? That is not good. That is not perfect. I must get everything into the distance; every ounce of energy I have should be expended in the race itself. I should be absolutely exhausted on the finish line. I should collapse over the tape, then and only then maybe I will have run a perfect race." I do think that is a great statement about acting.

The greatest theatre actors are fully drained after a very good performance. Other actors who should remain nameless only appear to be drained at a curtain call, which may give the impression that they have given their audience everything during the course of the evening.

There is a lesson in there about the timing of Clifford's death speech.

WHY: Well, there is a little of the news bulletin and the situation report here, is there not? A splendid final speech for the actor concerned, and for the character of Clifford. Having wished that the sun might not have been so charitable as to let Phaeton be in the driver's seat, Clifford curses the sun and his king. That King Henry was too lenient is Clifford's dying thought. He is finally redeemed by his admission of guilt, as he sees it, in supporting Henry VI.

WHERE: One of those areas of a battlefield to which men sometimes retreat and in which they too often die alone; the battlefields of the world may be at times very lonely places. Several people enter at the end of this speech, and there is only a brief moment here in which Clifford can make his final utterance and his peace. Is that a note from the author about pacing this speech? Probably. It certainly has to be borne in mind when playing the demise of Clifford. Over-prolonged death scenes are usually rather boring.

WHO: Clifford here is in a useful state of limbo for the actor. Somewhere between this life and the next he may talk to himself, to his God, to his widow. Of course, the speech if played in performance will be squeezed into a battle scene and out to an audience as a reminder that fighting a war is no joyful pastime.

OTHER: Watch the energy levels. This is a strong man who is mortally wounded and one who believes that he will not recover, that indeed he is close to death.
Clifford is correct in his conjecture. We discover that he has only sufficient strength remaining in this life to play

this speech. Maybe Clifford discovers the same thing along with the audience.

Glossary

LANCASTER, YORK two great dynasties of Northern England. These two families were the Hatfields and McCoys of the Wars of the Roses. There is to this day an annual cricket match between Yorkshire and Lancashire, which can get a little out of hand. Clifford was a Lancastrian.

PHOEBUS the sun.

BOOTLESS redundant.

PHAETON son of Helios. Reputed in mythology to have driven the sun's chariot for a day before being hit by a thunderbolt. This was of course before the days of learner driver's permits.

LENITY leniency, presumably on the part of the law.

PLAINTS complaints.

LET THOSE THAT
PLAY YOUR CLOWNS

Here follows a sample of comedic speeches. True,
not all of the following spring from the mouths
of "clowns" per se, but all, I think, could serve
some purpose in an audition.

As the "Advice" says more fully, "Let those that play your clowns speak no more than is set down for them, for there be of them that will themselves laugh, to set on some quantity of barren spectators to laugh too...." The author goes on to cite villainy and pitiful ambition in comics who are tempted to stoop too low for a cheap laugh.

Discretion is a word that may be used here too for the playing of comedy.

There are many traps, I think, in performing Bill's "comedy" monologues for auditions, for the very reason that the actor must take the speech out of context when, most often, only the context provides the comedic effect and not the speech itself.

The Porter in *Macbeth*, which we shall come to, is a case in point. The Porter's speech provides something of a relief from the butchery of the remainder of the play, but as a straightforward comedy speech it can be very tiresome if overplayed which, frankly, it almost always is in production.

I think any actor may take some consolation in the advice that specifically says clowns should "Speak no more than is set down for them." The plea from Hamlet and the author here is not, nor does it suggest, that the clown may not play off the text for comedic effect. On the contrary, it seems to me the fun of these pieces is often what the individual actor brings to them.

For exercise, you might like to take note of what Robin Williams actually says in a comedy stint. Often this brilliant comedian is not saying anything intrinsically funny. In Mr. Williams case it is the mania he brings to the mundane that provides such belly-aching laughter in his audiences. On the page, Mr. Williams's text might seem quite ordinary. He would be a wonderful Porter, I am sure.

Dennis Miller contorts a sentence to great comedic effect, no less than Mr. Williams contorts his body to our similar delight. Mr. Miller would clearly be a brilliant Touchstone in *As You Like It*, if he should choose to be.

Over the years many remarkable individuals have tackled the comedy of Bill's characters, in theatre and film and television. Invariably, it is the personality of the comic which brings the part home, sometimes with great success, but I have to admit there are times in one or two recent Shakespeare movies when the part does not seem to want to come home.

These following monologues can provide laughs, but, as Williams and Miller no doubt know, it takes extremely hard work.

If you want an easy path to an audition leave the comedy alone and stick to the more dramatic. It is said that on his deathbed Edmund Kean, the great English actor of the nineteenth century, was asked if he was all right. Kean raised himself up onto one elbow and said to his bedside companion, "Dying is easy. Comedy is hard."

The English music hall stand-up comedians Frankie Howerd, George Robey, Max Wall, and currently, Jim Dale, have over the years had signal success with some of the comedy roles in Bill's writing, as indeed have many good actors who are not noted solely for comedy: James Cagney, Derek Jacobi, Laurence Olivier, Ralph Richardson, Mickey Rooney, and Donald Sinden, to name but half a dozen. Often with these gentlemen it has been their introduction of bizarre body language that has aided their comedic effect. It is always the individual interpretation that will score.

The advice does not say that the actor may not bend the text, just that the actor should not add to the text. The advice to the players does not put a clamp on individualism; it merely attempts to keep the individual within the framework of the play, which is something I hold to be imperative.

ADRIANA

THE COMEDY OF ERRORS Act 2, Scene 2.
The Mart.
Enter Adriana

> *Adriana:* Ay, ay, Antipholus, look strange, and
>   frown:
> Some other mistress hath thy sweet aspects:
> I am not Adriana, nor thy wife.
> The time was once, when thou unurged wouldst
>   vow
> That never words were music to thine ear,
> That never object pleasing in thine eye,
> That never touch well welcome to thy hand,
> That never meat sweet-savoured in thy taste,
> Unless I spake, or looked, or touched, or carved to
>   thee.
> How comes it now, my husband, O, how comes it,
> That thou art then estrangèd from thyself?

Thyself I call it, being strange to me,
That, undividable, incorporate,
Am better than thy dear self 's better part.
Ah, do not tear away thyself from me;
For know, my love, as easy mayst thou fall
A drop of water in the breaking gulf,
And take unmingled thence that drop again,
Without addition or diminishing,
As take from me thyself, and not me too.
How dearly would it touch thee to the quick,
Shouldst thou but hear I were licentious!
And that this body, consecrate to thee,
By ruffian lust should be contaminate!
Wouldst thou not spit at me, and spurn at me,
And hurl the name of husband in my face,
And tear the stained skin off my harlot-brow,
And from my false hand cut the wedding-ring
And break it with a deep-divorcing vow?
I know thou canst - and therefore, see thou do it.
I am possessed with an adulterate blot,
My blood is mingled with the crime of lust:
For, if we two be one, and thou play false,
I do digest the poison of thy flesh,
Being strumpeted by thy contagion.
Keep then fair league and truce with thy true bed;
I live distained, thou undishonoured.

Adriana has been kept waiting for dinner and under-
stands that her husband, having been bidden, will not
come to her table. Frustrated, and accompanied by her sister, Adriana discovers her husband in the town, or so she

thinks. In fact, she is talking to her husband's twin brother, whom she has never met and about whom she knows nothing, not even of his existence.

Mistaken identity, of course. Funnier for the audience than for the character, maybe. Amusing stuff, to which Antipholus of Syracusa must react nonplussed.

Adriana has already expressed her concern to her sister, that her husband has fallen out of love with her, and here she goes for broke in an outright attack, albeit on the wrong man.

There is no doubt in Adriana's mind that this is her husband and that Dromio of Syracusa, at his side, is their servant.

Clearly such an outburst is not predicated solely on the fact that her husband is late for dinner. A long-festering boil is being lanced here. To no avail, as her husband, not being present, does not hear a word of the attack.

WHY: This is early in the play and the first time that the two masters become embroiled in a case of mistaken identity, as their two servants have already been. A huge crack being developed, which Bill will close with the mortar of great comedy before the end of the evening. Nice irony and intelligence from Adriana in suggesting that she must be "possessed with an adulterate blot" since she has been with her husband when he is obviously so tainted.

WHERE: Antipholus has earlier agreed to meet his servant on the Mart and we may suppose that having done his announced sightseeing around Ephesus, he is doing so. If it is the Mart, the location will influence Adriana's speech, since she is now attacking her husband in a public place and may attract some attention from passersby. I take it as a clue to her anger and frustration that she is willing to publicize the character of their married life. Again, it is not really her husband she is attacking, but she does not know that.

WHO: Adriana, directly to the man who she thinks is her husband. She includes his servant, who is also the twin of her own servant, and she is aided and abetted in her error by her sister Luciana. Regrettably the attack is at, and for the benefit of, the wrong Antipholus.

OTHER: So early in the play and after a little misunderstanding concerning the identity of the Dromio twins, the misunderstanding here of Adriana, who cannot properly identify her own husband, opens up enormous potential for the remaining comedy of mistaken identity. The more reason for Adriana to go for broke here.

Glossary

ANTIPHOLUS Adriana's husband.

LANCELOT GOBBO

THE MERCHANT OF VENICE Act 2, Scene 2.
A street in Venice.
Enter Lancelot Gobbo

Lancelot: Certainly my conscience will serve me to run from this Jew my master. The fiend is at mine elbow, and tempts me, saying to me, "Gobbo, Lancelot Gobbo, good Lancelot," or "good Gobbo," or "good Lancelot Gobbo, use your legs, take the start, run away." My conscience says, "No; take heed, honest Lancelot; take heed, honest Gobbo;" or, as aforesaid, "honest Lancelot Gobbo; do not run; scorn running with thy heels." Well, the most courageous fiend bids me pack, "Via!" says the fiend; "away!" says the fiend; "for the heavens, rouse up a brave mind," says the fiend, "and run." Well, my conscience, hanging about the neck of my heart, says very wisely to me, "My honest friend Lancelot, being an honest man's son,"- or rather an honest woman's son - for, indeed, my father did something smack, something grow to, he had a kind of taste; well, my conscience says, "Lancelot, budge not." "Budge," says the fiend. "Budge not," says my conscience. "Conscience," say I, "you counsel well." "Fiend," say I, "you counsel well." To be ruled by my conscience, I should stay with the Jew my master, who (God bless the mark!) is a kind of devil; and to run away from the Jew, I should be ruled by the fiend, who saving your reverence, is the devil himself. Certainly, the Jew is the very devil incarnation and, in my conscience, my conscience is but a kind of hard conscience, to offer to counsel me to stay with the Jew. The fiend gives the more friendly counsel: I will run, fiend. My heels are at your commandment, I will run.

Shylock's servant, Lancelot Gobbo, already wishes to leave the service of his master and here he is in a Venetian street contemplating what he should do, what course of action his so-called conscience dictates for him.

We will see very soon what real conscience Lancelot has, when almost immediately, his blind father appears in the same street looking to find his way, and the son sets out to play a cruel joke on his father.

The "conscience" speech provides a good opportunity for the actor to invent a persona for the devil, another persona for Shylock, and even one for his own conscience. Ample fabric here too, to move the speech, as Lancelot is talking about so many different people and points of view, all of which seem to be pulling and pushing him in one direction or another.

Gobbo knows he is a weak man, in fact he very soon reveals that his main thought about joining the household of Bassanio is that he might get a new uniform out of it. There is a great deal of fun to be had out of the repetition of his name throughout this speech. An interesting game in finding the right word for the actor to pounce on or to extend.

I have not mentioned "pouncing," and it needs a few words of explanation. It is the loading of a particular word, sometimes quite arbitrary and at the sole discretion of the actor making the phrase. Anthony Hopkins is a great exponent of the "pounce."

This remarkable actor learned in a good school of pouncing, and Sir Anthony might agree that he learned from an acknowledged master of the pounce, one Laurence Kerr Olivier.

I think the following anecdote is relevant and contains a good lesson. Olivier was once asked (he used to credit Albert Finney as the questioner) why it was that at the beginning of his stage performance of Richard III he took a seemingly extreme liberty with the pounce he made on the opening word, "NOW.......is the winter of our discontent..." Olivier explained to the younger actor that he had always been a little troubled by the fact that when "many people come into a theatre, they have difficulty finding their seats; they may have been shopping; they have had a look at the programme; auntie has opened her box of chocolates; they are all at sixes and sevens and I didn't want any of them to miss a single second of my brilliant performance, so I hit that first word and waited to make sure that I had everybody's full attention."

It is certainly true that Laurence Olivier made that statement and probably that was the truth of that particular pounce in Richard III. I think some people call it "pulling focus."

Whatever it is termed in today's market, the pounce is a wonderful tool for the stage actor, and Anthony Hopkins, Mr. Finney and others continue to make good use of it in other mediums.

WHY: In the play, the entrance and the character give us a distraction from the main plots of romance and money lending. Lancelot Gobbo's character takes the racism of the Christian Venetians to the serving classes and therefore to a wider front.

Shylock is being cut off on all sides, in preparation for the fall. Soon Bassanio will persuade Gobbo to leave Shylock. There is very little fidelity in this play, apart from that between Shylock and his friend Tubal.

WHERE: A street in Venice and therefore probably near putrid water. One imagines from Bassanio's entrance speech shortly after the Gobbo monologue that it is early afternoon. Certainly after a midday meal, as Bassanio's instructions to a departing servant are concerning the next meal at "five of the clock."

Incidentally Gobbo's character provides an interesting clue to the irresponsibility of Bassanio. Bassanio is flat broke at the beginning of the play, but he is still ordering servants concerning meals and new clothes and hiring yet another member for his staff. Portia's money will not last long, one suspects. Gobbo is not such a fool that he has not realized the pickings with Bassanio will be greater than they were with Shylock.

WHO: Direct attack at the audience, with whom Lancelot establishes an immediate contact and rapport. Particularly, it seems to me, the speech is played to the lower orders in the house, with whom Lancelot hopes to curry a little favour for his malpractice. Lancelot could hardly hope to get sympathy from the intellectuals or even the merchants in the audience; he is clearly nothing more nor less than a scoundrel, and even he knows that much about himself.

OTHER: Interesting that Gobbo thinks of Shylock as being a "kind of devil," but even Gobbo makes the distinction of having to apologize to his audience in the theatre, "saving your reverence" when he cites the actual "devil himself." Perhaps Gobbo is only trying to rationalize leaving Shylock. Gobbo's current position with Shylock certainly must be a cushy number, looking after Shylock and Jessica. Shylock is not a great entertainer, and there are only the two people in the house for whom Gobbo has to care.

Glossary

SMACK kiss.
GROW TO yes, well, exactly. Benny Hill humor. (What a great Gobbo Mr. Hill would have made!)
GOD BLESS THE MARK exclamation of the day, meaning "I hope I am right." "I trust." Actually, most likely a reference to the "mark" at the centre of an archery target, which the bowman hopes his shaft will hit.

TOUCHSTONE

AS YOU LIKE IT Act 5, Scene 3.
The Forest of Arden.
Enter Touchtone, Audrey, Jaques

Touchtone: Upon a lie seven times removed...bear
your body more seeming, Audrey...as thus, sir: I did
dislike the cut of a certain courtier's beard: he sent me
word, if I said his beard was not cut well, he was in
the mind it was: this is called the Retort Courteous. If
I sent him word again "it was not well cut," he would
send me word he cut it to please himself: this is called
the Quip Modest. If again, "it was not well cut," he
disabled my judgment; this is called the Reply
Churlish. If again, "it was not well cut," he would
answer I spake not true: this is call'd the Reproof
Valiant. If again, "it was not well cut," he would say I
lie: this is called the Countercheck Quarrelsome: and
so to the Lie Circumstantial and the Lie Direct.

(Jaques: And how oft did you say his beard was not well cut?)

I durst go no further than the Lie Circumstantial: nor he durst not give me the Lie Direct: and so we measured swords and parted.

(Jaques: Can you nominate in order now the degrees of the lie?)

O sir, we quarrel in print - by the book: as you have books for good manners.... I will name you the degrees. The first, the Retort Courteous; the second, the Quip Modest; the third, the Reply Churlish; the fourth, the Reproof Valiant; the fifth, the Countercheck Quarrelsome; the sixth, the Lie with Circumstance; the seventh, the Lie Direct... All these you may avoid, but the Lie Direct, and you may avoid that too, with an If. I knew when seven justices could not take up a quarrel, but when the parties were met themselves, one of them thought but of an If; as, "If you said so, then I said so," and they shook hands and swore brothers. Your If is the only peacemaker; much virtue in If.

Obviously, for the purposes of an audition you would cut the two lines of Jaques. A simple "But" may get the actor across the first bridge. For the second, perhaps a "You see sir, we quarrel in print" would work. You may well find a more comfortable way of joining the two speeches, but for an audition they are joinable.

Here is Touchstone, a classic court jester. A "fool," as Jaques repeatedly calls him in the play.

Having stated that he once had a quarrel that went to the seventh cause, Touchstone is asked by Jaques to describe the various stages which led to the seventh. While attempting to discipline the impassioned and unruly farm girl, Audrey, who is so infatuated with him, Touchstone gives to Jaques his account of the lineage of the argument. As he sets out the framework of courtly quarreling, Touchstone builds to the wonderful climax of the summary, in which, using great dexterity, he should be able to amuse and impress his seniors. As any actor might be able to impress and amuse a casting director, or producer with the deft manipulation of these speeches.

As you see I have boxed the dialogue into one speech here. I think it works as a means of demonstrating the verbal precision that any self respecting actor should attain.

Touchstone is acting here; at least it is fair to imagine that he has done this "routine" on many previous occasions. It is not something which he is improvising on the spur of the moment, but more likely one of his set pieces, which he has been polishing over the years. Therefore, as with those great riffs of Dennis Miller, Touchstone will know exactly where he is going within the speech. Unlike the comedy of Gobbo, which grows organically out of the moment, this description by Touchstone is the work of a skilled performer.

WHY: Purely showing off to impress those senior to him and because Touchstone so much enjoys making mock with the English language. Touchstone's relish for this, his last flourish in the play before getting married to the dreadful Audrey, is apparent. A symbolic bachelor party, perhaps, if one somewhat reduced in the numbers attendant at it.

WHERE: Somewhere around the Forest of Arden, in which almost the entire play is set.

WHO: Played pretty directly for Jaques and the duke, but there may well be a few other courtiers around, off whom Touchstone would be experienced enough to play.

OTHER: It is a mild joke that there should be such a thing as a book of bad manners, but Machiavelli had long been in print when Bill wrote *As You Like It*, and many people around the courts of Europe would have been writing and reading books concerning codes of conduct both good and bad.

Glossary

SEEMING It is for the actor, of course, but the mind boggles at what Audrey may be doing to cause Touchstone to interrupt himself here, at the outset.

DURST dare.

THE PORTER

MACBETH Act 2, Scene 3.
Macbeth's castle.
*The knocking grows louder: a drunken Porter
enters the court*

Porter: Here's a knocking, indeed! If a man were
porter of hell-gate he should have old turning the key.
(*knocking*) Knock, knock, knock! Who's there, i'th'-
name of Beelzebub? Here's a farmer, that hanged himself on th'expectation of plenty: come in, time-server;
have napkins enow about you, here you'll sweat for't.
(*knocking*) Knock, knock! Who's there, in th' other
devil's name? Faith, here's an equivocator, that could
swear in both the scales against either scale, who
committed treason enough for God's sake, yet could
not equivocate to heaven: O, come in, equivocator!
(*knocking*) Knock, knock, knock! Who's there? Faith,
here's an English tailor come hither for stealing out of

147

a French hose: come in, tailor; here you may roast your goose. (*knocking*) Knock, knock! Never at quiet! What are you? But this place is too cold for hell. I'll devil-porter it no further. I had thought to have let in some of all professions, that go the primrose way to th' everlasting bonfire. (*knocking*) Anon, anon! I pray you, remember the porter.

[Opens the gate]

(*Macduff*: Was it so late, friend, ere you went to bed that you do lie so late?)

Faith, sir, we were carousing till the second cock, and drink, sir, is a great provoker of three things.

(*Macduff*: What three things doth drink especially provoke?)

Marry, sir, nose-painting, sleep, and urine. Lechery, sir, it provokes, and unprovokes: it provokes the desire, but it takes away the performance. Therefore, much drink may be said to be an equivocator with Lechery: it makes him, and it mars him; it sets him on, and it takes him off; it persuades him and disheartens him; makes him stand to, and not stand to; in conclusion, equivocates him in a sleep, and, giving him the lie, leaves him.

NB: Delete bracketed lines for audition.

Many consider this to be the funniest monologue written for a low comedy player in the canon; many more might argue that it is one of the most awkward speeches from which to extract humor. The actors who play this speech are usually, in my experience, in the former group. Those who watch the speech being performed are invariably in the latter, as I have been, I regret, on too many occasions.

Again, MacDuff's two short speeches will not be used in auditions. Simply allow the Porter's to run on.

The Porter here is undeniably speaking great truths concerning the effects of alcohol, but I think the line to take is to pursue the truth of his situation and not to hunt around for cheap laughs. Then the speech could become a fascinating and humorous study in drunkenness, and clearly there is ample opportunity for an actor to show his talents in the pursuit of that image. If the people viewing the audition bust a gut laughing, so much the better.

Of course, it is not an accident on Bill's part that this drunken man imagines that he is portering the gates of hell. The Porter does not know that Duncan has just been murdered but we do, and that the whole house will this day quickly become a hell on earth for those inside it.

The Porter's attitude also epitomizes the relaxed security around Glamis Castle, which partly enabled the regicide of Duncan in the first place.

WHY: To provide MacDuff with an entrance; to establish that the house is unaware of the murder; to relax the atmosphere with an attempt at humor immediately prior to the discovery of Duncan's murdered body.

WHERE: An outer gate of the castle; early morning. Too early for the Porter.

WHO: The Porter speaks much of the time to himself here, but again with the potential to play to the audience in the theatre with his reverie. Drunks, you may have observed, often invent people to talk to, or better still, talk to themselves as if they were someone else. In a modern context the Porter could play some of this speech to a wall mirror.

OTHER: It is interesting to note in the first section of the speech that the lines are full of images of death and disaster: "a farmer, that hanged himself," "committed treason," "roast your goose," "everlasting bonfire." Everywhere in this play, the characters seem to be surrounded by, or giving voice to, the darkest imagery; even here in what may be intended as a light respite from the tragedy of the main plot, there is a dark quality.

Does the Porter have trouble finding his clothes? Is he dressed? Perhaps he has on only one boot. What does he drink? Whom does he drink with?

Glossary

COURT (SD) courtyard.
BEELZEBUB the devil.
ENOW enough.

LAUNCE

THE TWO GENTLEMEN OF VERONA
Act 2, Scene 3.
Verona: a street.
Launce approaches, leading a dog

Launce: Nay, 'twill be this hour ere I have done weeping; all the kind of the Launces have this very fault.... I have received my proportion, like the Prodigious Son, and am going with Sir Proteus to the Imperial's court....I think Crab, my dog, be the sourest-natured dog that lives; my mother weeping, my father wailing; my sister crying; our maid howling; our cat wringing her hands; and all our house in a great perplexity- yet did not this cruel-hearted cur shed one tear; he is a stone, a very pebble-stone, and has no more pity in him than a dog; a Jew would have wept to have seen our parting: why, my grandam, having no eyes, look you, wept herself blind at my parting: nay, I'll show you the manner of it.....This shoe is my father.....no, this left shoe is my father, no, no, this left shoe is my mother.....nay, that cannot be so neither.....yes; it is so, it is so; it hath the worser sole... this shoe, with the hole in it, is my mother, and this my father.....a vengeance on't! there 'tis... Now, sir, this staff is my sister; for, look you, she is as white as a lily and as small as a wand: this hat is Nan, our maid: I am the dog......no, the dog is himself, and I am the dog.....O, the dog is me, and I am myself: ay: so, so....Now come I to my father; "Father, your blessing;" now should not the shoe speak a word for weeping: now should I kiss my father; well, he weeps on....Now come I to my mother: O, that she could speak now, like a wood woman: well, I kiss her: why there 'tis; here's my mother's breath up and down....Now come I to my sister; mark the moan she makes...now the dog all this while sheds not a tear; nor speaks a word: but see how I lay the dust with my tears.

I think it is customary to use the character of Launce in this play for the purposes of auditioning; however, many people choose Launce's speech from the beginning of Act 4, Scene 4. Certainly that speech is worth a look, but I offer the thought here of using this introductory speech of Launce because it is the beginning of the character, and as such, it is, I think, inherently more useful for an audition. Generally speaking, the less you have to explain about what you are about to do in an audition context the better. Many of the speeches in this book are the character's opening words and therefore require nothing but a simple announcement of the character and the play.

Launce has a characteristic later in the play of misinterpreting the English spoken to him. "Tied" for "tide" being the first example in the next dialogue with Panthino, and "mastership" for "Master's ship" and so on. Here is a good chance then to see the man and to assess the mind with which he is equipped. Does Launce understand that he makes such errors? Does he enjoy what might be feeble attempts at wordplay? The pedantry of the problem outlined here, namely, which shoe should depict which parent, is also an interesting key to character.

Again, this speech is virtually a blank sheet upon which the actor may begin to sketch the character. It is possible here to outline for the audience what aspects of comedy they should be attuned to in the remainder of the play.

As is the case with many of these low comedy characters, Launce is a very real person indeed. It is not, I think, a question of how to tell the joke of the comedy, so much as it is how to express the truthful dilemma of the person. There are one or two "jokes," of course, "my grandam having no eyes, look you, wept herself blind," and the like.

The insistence on the shoe with the hole in it as being representative of his mother is another cheap shot, but what gives the character life and vitality and makes us want to watch him for the rest of the evening is his humanity and the manner in which he expounds about a situation (leaving home), with which we are all quite familiar. Again this author immediately creates a bond between a character and the audience.

WHY: Get the character onto the stage. Establish that damned dog. Pursue the plot. With Panthino leaving imme-

diately before this entrance of Launce and returning immediately after this speech, there is a passage of time marked
out for us and a change of pace. There is, too, the point
here that this speech follows so closely the departure of
Proteus, Launce's master. Proteus has just commented on
the lack of tears in his recent parting and has been shov-
eled off the scene and the stage by the seemingly busy
Panthino.

Launce seems somehow to be reluctant to leave for
Milan. At least he is not in any hurry. He very quickly
becomes comfortable with the speech, and hopefully with
the audience.

WHERE: If Julia and Proteus were parting close to Julia's
home, as they seem so recently to have done, then it seems
probable that this following scene may be in a similar area.
It must be quite close to the dock, too, as Panthino seems
to have been to the ship with Proteus and is now back to
gather Launce.

OTHER: One of the funniest vaudeville acts I ever saw
was that fine comedian in *Sugar Babies* who had a highly
trained dog which did absolutely nothing that his master
asked of him. The risk of taking even such a well-trained
dog to an audition is that the animal may get work and
you may not, unless you can obtain a bite of the percent-
age.

Age is an interesting dilemma for the actor playing Launce.
The character is often played as an older man, but if we
are to believe him, his mother and father are still alive, he
still seems to be subservient to Panthino: he is referred

to as a "madcap," albeit by a "sweet youth" referred to as a "boy," though Launce, too, refers to Speed as a boy. Launce might be in his late twenties or early thirties. Whatever his age, we know that he finishes the scene in tears, since Panthino comes on immediately the speech is over and tells us so.

Glossary

PRODIGIOUS SON prodigal son.
MARK notice.

POMPEY

MEASURE FOR MEASURE Act 4, Scene 3.
Another room in the prison.

Pompey enters

Pompey: I am as well acquainted here as I was in
our house of profession: one would think it were
Mistress Overdone's own house, for here be many of
her old customers.... First, here's young Master Rash;
he's in for a commodity of brown paper and old gin-
ger- nine-score and seventeen pounds, of which he
made five marks, ready money: marry then ginger was
not much in request, for the old women were all
dead....Then is there here one Master Caper, at the
suit of Master Three-pile the mercer, for some four
suits of peach-coloured satin, which now peaches him
a beggar...Then have we here young Dizzy, and young
Master Deepvow, and Master Copperspur, and
Master Starvelackey, the rapier and dagger man, and

young Dropheir that killed lusty Pudding, and Master Forthright the tilter, and brave Master Shoetie, the great traveller, and wild Halfcan that stabbed Pots, and, I think, forty more - all great doers in our trade, and are now 'for the Lord's sake.'

Pompey, finding himself in prison, makes a comparison between the gaol and the bawdy house, where he was recently employed by Mistress Overdone.

This speech becomes something of what could be referred to as a list, but it is a list with comedy potential if the actor can build it properly. Of course, the speech carries some exposition, in that we are reminded that we are still in the prison, though probably in a different location within the prison from the previous scene.

Necessary passage of time too, as Barnardine's head has just been ordered and the author is covering that aspect with the use of Pompey here.

It is quite common for Bill to put a comedian out there on that thrust stage to hold the audience between more relevant matters. Just as we use comedians today: Billy Crystal linking the elements of the Oscar awards ceremony. Such an assignment is a testing ground for any comedy player, and sometimes it proves too difficult, even for the best, to keep to the strictures of the linking role.

The great English postwar comics Tony Hancock, Frankie Howerd, Max Miller, Spike Milligan, Derek Roy, Peter Sellars, Kenneth Williams, among others, all maintained that they became good at stand-up because they were given the exacting task of "filling in" at the Windmill Theatre in London's West End. Their task at the "Open-

Twenty-Four-Hours" Windmill was to keep the so-called raincoat brigade amused for five minutes or so between the various nude *tableaux vivants* which were the main fare of that most prestigious music hall theatre. Vamping not till ready, but till the ladies of the chorus were unclothed and in the case of the Windmill Girls, stationary. The British censors did not allow nudes on stage to move. The same official office that licensed Elizabethan plays still licensed all English drama until 1968, when the Lord Chamberlain's office gave up the ghost, and English plays were finally no longer subject to censorship. As a bonus, nudes were free to move around the stage.

In Bill's case he often places a similar burden on his low comedy players, in that he gives them somewhat indifferent material and asks them to hold the fort until the plot may proceed. If you can get laughs with some of this stuff you are a very imaginative comedian, but as I have said, the laughter will probably come from what you do, and the manner in which you speak the lines, rather than the lines themselves.

WHY: As suggested, Pompey has to hold us until we can proceed. Interesting parallel between the brothel and the gaol. Lovely cast of characters for anyone even remotely interested in words.

WHERE: The prison in Vienna. Depending on the production design and the style of the company, the prison may be anything from a dank, dark, Bastille-like dungeon, to something in plastic and aluminum. Despite the elegant lines Mr. Lovelace once wrote, prison is prison, whether with garden walls, or iron cages.

WHO: In dramatic reality, Pompey is here talking to himself, but any actor is doubtless very pleased to have his character overheard by the theatre audience, with whom he is by now confident.

OTHER: Interesting to determine how and where and when and why Pompey knows all of the people to whom he refers in this little speech. I personally would want to work out why Pompey thinks he can get a laugh out of a reference to "lusty Pudding," even though I know there is such a thing as a lusty pudding and that it is quite funny to talk of Mr. Pudding in this context of murder as having been lusty. Is Pompey deliberately making a weak joke? That is an art of comedy. Johnny Carson had such a technique; in fact, I think Mr. Carson was a master of riding a weak joke or exploiting a joke that misfired. Jay Leno is not quite so strong in that suit, though he certainly deploys it from time to time. A good or experienced comedian will be able to take a laugh on, and to help it build, even though the initial joke was a weak joke. The vulnerability good comics allow themselves in such moments often helps them with the remainder of their material. The same vulnerability, and the awareness of it, is, I think, what makes some stand-up comedians such worthwhile actors. To act well, you almost always need to be aware of your vulnerability and of the vulnerability of the character you are playing. Certainly from my limited experience with stand-up comedy it is all too easy to feel completely naked out there in the middle of the stage. Such a feeling may, however, in turn provide a great source of energy if the actor can harness it.

Glossary

FIVE MARKS monetary denomination. A mark was
about two thirds of a pound sterling. Perhaps a reasonable gratuity.

GINGER considered by many to have an aphrodisiac
quality.

MISTRESS QUICKLY

HENRY V Act 2, Scene 3.
London: before a tavern.
Enter Pistol, Nym, Bardolph, Boy, and Hostess
(Mistress Quickly)

Mistress Quickly: Nay sure, he's not in hell: he's in
Arthur's bosom, if ever man went to Arthur's bosom:
'a made a finer end, and went away an it had been
any christom child: 'a parted e'en just between twelve
and one, e'en at the turning o' th' tide: for after I saw
him fumble with the sheets, and play with flowers,
and smile upon his finger's end, I knew there was but
one way: for his nose was as sharp as a pen, and 'a
babbled of green fields. "How now, Sir John?" quoth
I. "What, man! be o' good cheer:" so 'a cried out
"God, God, God!" three or four times: now I, to com-
fort him, bid him 'a should not think on God: I hoped

there was no need to trouble himself with any such thoughts yet: so 'a bade me lay more clothes on his feet: I put my hand into the bed, and felt them, and they were as cold as any stone: then I felt to his knees, and so up'ard and up'ard, and all was as cold as any stone.

Yes, you're right. I think so too. It is fair to argue that Mistress Quickly is not strictly speaking a clown, but the character demonstrates elsewhere a great talent for creating mirth and laughter, and here the lady seems to be quite unable to deny the humor and bawdiness of her personality, even though she is describing with great feeling the death of her friend and onetime bed partner, Sir John Falstaff. It is, I think, an interesting example of how one might take the edge off an otherwise tragic moment. The comedic potential in the speech seems to be irresistible to the elderly inn hostess.

The speech is another example of this author's striking hard through the mouth of a clownish figure. Perhaps that is one of the reasons Bill, and Hamlet, are so adamant that there should be a tight discipline exacted on the playing of comedy in the plays. This death of Falstaff was a most important death, both for the play and for the audience attending those early performances of *Henry V*. It must have been expertly played to have prevented a riot, so beloved was the character the author was killing off. In recent times some may recall the last episode of *MASH* on television and the ensuing press coverage. With the death of Falstaff there is something of the same circumstance. A large public felt some sense of loss in both instances. The death of Falstaff, albeit offstage, was a crippling blow for the theatregoing audience of Elizabethan London when they first heard of it. So great was the loss, we are reliably informed, that the queen commissioned her pet playwright to reincarnate the old knight Sir John. The roguish character was brought back to the boards for one more play; hence we have the rather-less-than-satisfactory Falstaff depicted in *The Merry Wives of Windsor*.

This speech needed very careful handling. As did the body of the dying old Sir John, or so Mistress Quickly would have us believe. If actors go only for the physical outward show of the comedy, for what is the easy initial laugh, and do not play the text truthfully, they will be inclined to miss such moments as this of Mistress Quickly. Too many times in the theatre, the eye of the audience is encouraged to look before its ear is invited to listen and the results are often, as I have observed, unsatisfactory.

WHY: The great character of Falstaff is completed here in this play, or so the author thought when he wrote the scene. As I said, Sir John was reinvented for *The Merry Wives of Windsor*. Given the ultimate royal pardon. Brought back by popular demand, as it were.

As the author wrote it, though, it was very fitting that Mistress Quickly, who had been there through much of the life of Falstaff, at least as depicted by Bill, should have the last relevant words in this account of his death. The speech serves as a most timely reminder to the troops leaving for another war: that death, on the battlefield or no, comes to us all. It may be stretching a point, I acknowledge, to refer to Pistol, Nym, the Boy, and Bardolph as "troops," but this bizarre quartet were strangely representative of the somewhat ragtag fighting force Henry took into this French campaign.

WHERE: Outside the inn in which, presumably, Falstaff has recently died. Mistress Quickly bidding the bizarre quartet of patrons and friends adieu; bidding her great passion in this life a long, tearful, and wryly humorous farewell.

WHO: Just a reported speech to those gathered, some of which number will be likely to die, or come near to death, in France.

OTHER: Mistress Quickly has already by this time passed on to the bed of Pistol, but the fraternity does not seem to object to her loving, tender eulogy over Falstaff.

Speaking of "clowns," in the Olivier film of *Henry V*, Falstaff is seen, which he is not intended to be, I think, in the play. Laurence Olivier, himself a truly brilliant comic actor, cast the great English music hall comedian George Robey in the part of the dying Falstaff. That particular casting of Robey was a typical and heartfelt compliment from Olivier to a whole generation of comedians whom he admired. Olivier, of all actors, knew that Kean was right about death being easy, comedy being hard.

Glossary

ARTHUR'S BOSOM paradise.
CHRISTOM CHILD child dying so young that he or she would be buried in their christening robes.
ALL WAS AS COLD AS ANY STONE.......Dear old soul, isn't she? The question for the actor is, do you go for the comedy implied in the line, or for the tragic implications of the death? May you catch both?

VIOLA

TWELFTH NIGHT Act 2, Scene 2.
A street near Olivia's house.
Enter Viola, Malvolio following

Viola: I left no ring with her: what means this lady?
Fortune forbid my outside have not charmed her!
She made good view of me, indeed so much,
That sure methought her eyes had lost her tongue,
For she did speak in starts distractedly....
She loves me, sure - the cunning of her passion
Invites me in this churlish messenger....
None of my lord's ring! why, he sent her none...
I am the man - if it be so, as 'tis,
Poor lady, she were better love a dream....
Disguise, I see thou art a wickedness,
Wherein the pregnant enemy does much.
How easy is it for the proper-false

In women's waxen hearts to set their forms!
Alas, our frailty is the cause, not we,
For such as we are made of, such we be....
How will this fadge? My master loves her dearly,
And I (poor monster!) fond as much on him:
And she, mistaken, seems to dote on me:
What will become of this? As I am man,
My state is desperate for my master's love;
As I am woman -now alas the day!-
What thriftless sighs shall poor Olivia breathe?
O Time, thou must untangle this, not I,
It is too hard a knot for me t' untie.

Hardly a clown, Viola, but here is a light comedy mono-logue that requires a sensitive touch and one which will certainly illustrate any comedy potential the actor might want to exhibit. Interesting problem in establishing, main-taining, and sustaining the surprise Viola has registered with her use of disguise. Viola is at once intrigued, delight-ed, and maybe a little amazed that the situation with Olivia has developed.

A pleasant voyage of discovery and slight amusement, playing on the pronounced theme of love, which was marked at the beginning of the play.

Ample opportunity to color the character of Viola and propel the plot along at the same time. Great possibility with "How will this fadge?"and "What will become of this?" to comment not only upon the line and the situation, but on the character of Viola.

WHY: Develop the plot. Engage the mistaken identity

and mistaken gender theme for the brunt of the play. Demonstrate Viola's sense of humor and enjoyment at not dealing directly with the problem represented by the offer of the ring.

WHERE: The location is not specific, except to say it sounds probable that Malvolio, who has just delivered the ring is not too far away from his mistress's home: "Even now...On a moderate pace I have arrived but hither." Perhaps Viola is taking a short cut back across a meadow. My edition has the scene set in "A street," but much as I hate to disagree with the great eruditon and expertise of Mr. Dover Wilson, I don't fully understand such a limitation.

WHO: Musing very much to herself, Viola is not speaking directly to the audience in the theatre but is in another limbo, or no-man's-land, in which we can all imagine that the character is indeed talking to us in the auditorium.

OTHER: She does of course pick the ring up, else there would be no ensuing play. I haven't mentioned short versions in this text, but here is an opportunity to do so. I have often played the game of the "short version" of the play. What would happen were Othello not to recall that he had given his wife a handkerchief with a strawberry mark embroidered on it? Might Othello then simply reply in the negative when he is asked the question by Iago? The play, as we know it, can hardly proceed, and the play would become altogether different. Similarly, here, with Viola, it would be tempting to take the direction of Malvolio's last speech in the scene: "There it lies in your eye; if not, be it his that finds it." It would change the plot more than a little if Viola were to leave the ring upon the ground and some total stranger were to pick it up. A clear case of unspoken stage direction from the author. Bill does not need to give the stage direction "Viola picks up ring and exits." The delightful resolution to the problem is left for the actor. Where does Viola pick up the ring? On what line? With what intention?

Glossary

FADGE turn out, develop.

That is all, for the moment.

I hope this book "fadges" well for you, or rather, I hope your auditions and performances all "fadge" well, and that this book will be of some assistance to that end....

Thank you, William, whoever you were.

Thank you, reader, wherever you are.

As "Mr. Shakespeare" said through the mouth of Hamlet, "Go, make you ready."